FINDING YOUR PEOPLE

FINDING YOUR PEOPLE

The ultimate guide to friendship

**Alexandra Hourigan
& Sally McMullen**
of *Two Broke Chicks*

PEOPLE

ALLEN&UNWIN
SYDNEY • MELBOURNE • AUCKLAND • LONDON

First published in 2024

Allen & Unwin
Cammeraygal Country
83 Alexander Street
Crows Nest NSW 2065
Australia
Phone: (61 2) 8425 0100
Email: info@allenandunwin.com
Web: www.allenandunwin.com

Allen & Unwin acknowledges the Traditional Owners of the Country on which we live and work. We pay our respects to all Aboriginal and Torres Strait Islander Elders, past and present.

A catalogue record for this book is available from the National Library of Australia

ISBN 978 1 76147 042 4

Cover design by George Saad
Illustrations by Mika Tabata
Text design by Bookhouse, Sydney
Set in 12.5/17.6 pt Minion Pro by Bookhouse, Sydney

10 9 8 7 6 5 4 3 2 1

The paper in this book is FSC® certified. FSC® promotes environmentally responsible, socially beneficial and economically viable management of the world's forests.

*For all the friends who have inspired this book
and all the new friends we have yet to meet*

CONTENTS

SOOOO, DO YOU WANNA BE FRIENDS?

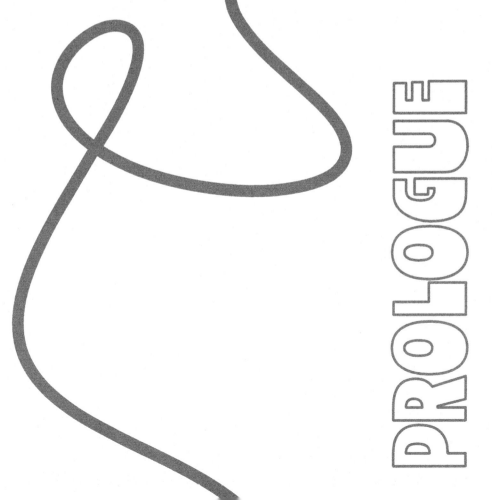

PROLOGUE

No matter where you are in life, you haven't yet met all the people who will love you. This book was written to help you find them.

Friends are the people you call after the worst first date you've ever had.

Friends are the people who sit on the couch with you, hungover as hell, and order you a Maccas hash brown without you even asking.

Friends are the people who are just as happy as you are when you get that promotion you deserve.

Most importantly, friends are the people who love you—warts, shitty ex-partners, irrational meltdowns and all. They see you for who you are.

Friendships give us the opportunity to learn and grow into new versions of ourselves and evolve through different eras of our lives. Friendships can also be fickle, fleeting and full of drama. Sometimes these challenges can help a relationship evolve, or they can help us learn what we do (and don't) want out of the connections in our life. We always say that out of every friendship, good or bad, there's a life lesson to be learned. No friendship is ever a waste of time.

At our most primal level, humans need community and social interaction to survive. A Harvard University study found that friendship can extend our life expectancy. Research published in the *European Heart Journal Open* proved that friendship can lower the risk of heart failure.

We quite literally need friends to live.

Biology aside, friends are the main characters of our core memories. They're the other halves that make us whole. True friends call us out on our bullshit. They give us the gentle (but essential) roastings that we like to think are character-building. They're the ones who make our belly hurt from laughing, and fill the memories we didn't plan to make but are so happy to have.

Most importantly, friendship means we belong to someone. We belong to them because they chose us.

While friends fuel our mental and emotional wellbeing it is naive to think one person can serve all our needs. As the saying goes, people come into our lives for a reason, a season or a lifetime. They may not stick around forever, but friendships serve a purpose in all situations. Friendship can also bring light to life's heavy moments. The days when you're feeling low your friends are there to pick you up and dust you off. They are the source of belly laughs, stupid memories that make you smile and an unconditional love that makes you feel like the last piece of the puzzle has been slotted into place.

Maintaining friendships is much more complex than ordering our Myspace top friends list or increasing our Snapchat streak score. Not all friendships are roses, sparkles and unicorn farts. They can be hard work and include many ups and downs. Not all of them make it to the end of time, and that's okay. Think of the friend you went out partying with when you were single who you now barely speak to; the childhood friend who lives in a different city; or the friend you fell out with, but at least in the process you learned how to ask for what you need from people and stick up for yourself.

All friendships are different and bring you life experiences that build who you are as a person and as a friend, while teaching you what you value in others.

The Seven Friend Theory is a helpful tool to have in your back pocket while you're reading this book and considering the friendships in your life. This theory states that you need seven different types of friends to serve different purposes:

① a friend you've had since you were little
② a friend who can make you laugh in any situation
③ a friend you can go forever without talking to but nothing changes
④ a friend you can tell anything to
⑤ a friend who's like a sibling
⑥ a friend you can't imagine not being friends with
⑦ a friend who knows about all your relationship problems, even though they don't want to hear about them.

When you read this list you may immediately panic with the thought, 'But I don't have these seven types of friends!' Don't worry, many people reading this book will have that same realisation—you're not alone in that.

What we like about this theory is that it highlights how different connections can feed you, and that there's no one size that fits all when it comes to friends. You may have a friend who slots into four of the seven categories as well as a friend who personifies just one category—and that's the point.

This book is for people looking to find their *Sex and the City* core four, their *Friends* solid six . . . the Sally to their Alex, if you will. It's for people who don't know how to relinquish themselves from the toxic friendship they've had since primary school. It's for people who are grappling with the hard choice of whether a friendship is worth reviving from the operating table. It's for people who are wondering how the hell you make new friends as an adult. It's for people who are on the hunt for their platonic soulmate. Most importantly, it's for people who want to foster the most important friendship of all: the one with themselves.

For the next ten chapters, please consider us your new best friends. We'll guide you through the tumultuous world of finding, building and developing friendships with people who are worth the love you have to give, and give you the love you deserve in return.

As a wise person once said nearly as well as we can: 'Truly great friends are hard to find, difficult to leave, and imposs-ible to forget.' No matter which part of that quote you identify with most strongly right now, this book will help navigate the rewarding yet sometimes messy nature of friendships. It's your step-by-step guide to finding your people and nurturing your connections with them—and yourself.

Lezgo.

So, who are we?

'I like your jeans!'

The four words that started it all. A friendship that would give Thelma and Louise a run for their money. Except their names are Alex Hourigan and Sally McMullen—that's us, by the way. We're two journalists who became literal soulmates, twin flames or whatever other Shakespearean term you want to throw at us.

It started in our early twenties when we met in the office kitchen. Six months later, we had our first set of matching tattoos and a bond that made the Pope sit up in bed in a cold sweat. Since then we've been through our fair share of highs, and some lows. The experience has taught us everything we wanted to know, needed to know and sometimes didn't want to face about friendships.

Look, we don't throw around the term 'experts'—but . . . we do. If you could have a qualification in friendship, we'd have PhDs. In our years together we've been through messy break-ups, workplace struggles, high school friendship breakdowns, third wheeling and international trips. We've learned lessons, good and bad, such as how to respect that we both have relationships beyond our own and that these don't take away from what we have together. The best part of life is finding multiple avenues to fulfil and challenge you—that's exactly what having different friendships does.

A note from Sal

Howdy, I'm Sal—the spicy Pisces of the pair. I was never one of the popular gals or part of a clique, but I've always been a social butterfly and valued friendship above pretty much everything else. Growing up in a tiny house with two older siblings on a street full of ratbag kids, there was probably no other way I could turn out.

If forced to describe me as a friend, I think my pals would say: empathetic, loyal and unafraid to dish out liberal servings of tough love. I have been known to defend my friends till the bitter end (even when they're in the wrong) and I'm not afraid to whip out the bullshit card (much to the dismay of many of my friends' exes).

My tendency to share my two cents to protect the people I love isn't always a good thing, though. I'm not a perfect friend by any means and have had my fair share of friendship break-ups. In fact, my first real experience of heartbreak involved a best friend in Year 7. We'll get into that later.

With Al by my side, I'm qualified to write this guide because the people I consider my ride-or-dies represent the different forms in which friendship can shapeshift. They include bonds fostered in the primary school playground, squished in sweaty mosh pits as a teen, on dirty dance floors in dive bars or in the humble office kitchen (as was the case with Al). I believe that no two friendships look the same, but they can all be beautiful and life-changing in their own weird ways.

Anyway, enough from me. Let me pass the mic over to my partner in crime.

A note from Al

Hey friend, I'm Alex, Ali, Hourigan and a mountain of other nicknames I've been bestowed in my lifetime but, really, my friends just call me Al.

I like to think of myself as a bit of a friendship chameleon. The friendships in my life have taken so many different pathways and forms and it's truly how I like it.

8

I grew up watching (aka obsessing over) 1990s and early 2000s television shows featuring iconic friendship duos, and yearning for the day that I'd have a witty comrade with whom I would share all life has to offer. Side by side we'd sneak out, move out and make out through our teens to our twenties.

However, like a lot of us, I didn't find friendship the easiest of pathways in my younger years. I fell into the 'popular' aka 'mean girl' group before becoming their next prey, and went through a best friend break-up that rocked me to my core. But in my late twenties I truly found my people, both on purpose and by accident. Let's just say I've done my fair share of learning.

Many of us believe that friendships should be easy, and that we simply stumble upon them. We think that on our first day of school a total stranger will approach us and, bam, we're best friends for life. Unfortunately, life is not like *Girl Meets World*.

My experience of friendship has been challenging but rewarding. I've learned that friendships are sometimes impermanent, but that's not necessarily a bad thing. I've learned that accidental, unexpected friendships are often the ones that have a place in your life forever. I've learned that you can make new friends at any point in your life, and that your age does not define you. I've learned that being my own best friend is just as important as finding others to connect with.

Most of all, I'm excited to be on this journey with you, gorgeous reader. I'm excited that because you're reading this, you're wanting to foster your friendships, become your own best friend, ditch the toxicity in your life and find your people.

You, Sal and I, over the next few hundred pages, are going to do exactly that.

While it took a few months for us to grow from work acquaintances to glued at the hip, when it did happen . . . hoo boy. It was a cosmic collision that gave the big bang a run for its money. We went from chatting in the office kitchen or grabbing the occasional coffee to multiple sleepovers a week, the aforementioned (planned) matching tattoos and (unplanned) matching outfits, and permanent residency at every dive bar in Sydney most Friday nights. It had probably only been around six months by this stage, but we felt like we had known each other for years. Or that, at the very least, our friendship was destined in the stars. Who else was a weird hybrid of an introverted extrovert and obsessed with Disney, Dad Rock and spicy penne arrabiata (extra olives please)? Nobody but us. It truly felt like a friendship of fate.

Together we've experienced a lot of milestones in individual friendships but also with one another. As much as we are each other's person, we too have experienced some peaks and valleys of friendship. What good friendship hasn't?

We now run a podcast called *Two Broke Chicks* in which, funnily enough, the subject of friendship comes up in every other episode. Over time, our DMs have become filled with questions from our listeners—whom we playfully call our chicks—about how to find friends in your twenties, how to spot the red flags of toxic friendships and how to navigate a friend who has suddenly become obsessed with their new partner. As we spoke about these issues on the podcast we realised that, while the stories we were sharing about our own lives were very personal to us, our audience felt seen, heard and validated by them. While the details may have been different, a lot of the feelings our listeners were experiencing and questions they were asking were almost identical to our own. We started to realise just how important (and sometimes bloody hard) it is to talk openly and honestly about the most critical relationships in our lives. We wanted to create a safe space for all of us to figure it out together, and this book is it. Consider it your backstage pass to our Instagram DMs.

Just like with friendships, you can navigate this book in whatever way you choose—whether you want to devour it cover to cover or pick and choose which chapters you want to hang out with when you feel like it. Maybe you just got into a new romantic relationship and need some advice on how to navigate your friendship group around it? Chapter 7 is now your new best friend. Maybe you're in your late twenties or adulthood and wanting to expand your friendship circle but have no idea how? Don't worry, we go into that too in Chapter 4.

However you choose to peruse this book, it's here for the long haul—as are we. We'll have your back and guide you through the different eras of friendship, whenever they happen and however they manifest.

BE YOUR OWN BESTIE

It may seem odd to start a book about friendship with a chapter on being alone, but bear with us here. We'll show you how the friendship you have with yourself is the most fruitful of all, and how it has a flow-on effect to all other relationships in your life—be they romantic, familial or platonic.

We all know what it means to have a stereotypical best friend. You know their quirky habits, weird likes and dislikes and innermost secrets. They're the person with whom you celebrate your wins, and the one you lean on during setbacks.

Now imagine this person is you.

Imagine how powerful you could be if you knew you had a best friend you could rely on, within yourself.

On top of the completely mind-blowing revelation you're likely having right now, you should also know that being alone sets the scene for the most beautiful friendships you could hope for. Yes, we get how backwards that sounds, but trust the process.

When you're your own best friend, you learn more about all the things you hold valuable in life, which allows you to navigate friendships like a pro. You understand what you want and need from your connections, and you appreciate all the positives you bring to other people's lives.

Once your cup is full of self-love, you have overflow to share with others.

It's a common (and incorrect) notion, especially for women, that if you love yourself you're vain, egotistical and arrogant. This false idea limits our individual growth and feeds the narrative that our worth is sourced externally.

While a haircut, a good flirt or an online shopping delivery can have you throwing it back on cloud nine, these things are purely that: *things*. They are fleeting, impermanent dopamine hits of happiness that do not last forever. When we believe our worth is sourced externally it becomes a measure of the objects we own, the size of our bank account, our physical appearance and, of course, others' opinions. When, really, the only measurement of self-worth should come from within.

Inner self-worth is like a muscle that needs to be trained. The longer we ignore it, the more the empty well within us grows. In vain, we attempt to fill this emotional well with shallow forms of validation such as others' approval, the number of social media followers we have, or ownership of the latest 'viral' or 'trending' product, because these things feel easier to attain than genuine self-love. It doesn't hurt that society puts a greater emphasis on chasing such things over fostering a healthy relationship with ourselves.

To think positively about ourselves is no easy task. We aren't built to wake up in the morning and think, 'Wow, I'm great, kind, smart and absolutely smokin' hot!' After years of seeing photoshopped beauty commercials and living in a society of trending body types, we're all a bit fucking confused as to what we're supposed to like about ourselves. In short, it's not your fault if you don't love yourself, but it *is* your responsibility to do something about it.

So rather than giving yourself an overly critical self-evaluation, start talking to yourself as you would your closest friend.

Because that is what you are. You are your own bestie. The person who is the 100 per cent constant in your life; the one who will always be there.

Start to ask yourself, 'Would I say that to my best friend?' (We'll take a wild guess and say the answer is probably 'No.') You wouldn't play judge, jury and executioner for a friend just because they made a human mistake, had a couch day, forgot to put their washing away or got a little too excited on a night out and now have the world's worst hangover. So stop condemning yourself with that gavel.

We're all individuals with our own internal monologue, weird habits, needs, secrets and loves. No one can ever truly know us as well as we know ourselves.

In life, you can be sure that you'll be bound by one thing: yourself. We use the word 'bound' because your connection with yourself is unbreakable and constant. You can never choose to not be with yourself. You are always there with your inner thoughts, feelings, insecurities and needs.

That may sound overwhelming, but it's why your friendship with yourself is the most important relationship of all. You're bound to the way you feel, see and treat yourself. You will live a much happier life once you realise you can *choose* to be the best friend you've always wanted for yourself.

There's no doubt that our relationships with others, whether platonic, romantic or familial, are life-changing and soul-fulfilling. But it's our connection with ourselves that is the one thing we can count on in our lives. So why is it the one we most often neglect? Through the fattest tears you've shed, the biggest cackles you've unleashed and the most embarrassing moments you've cringed through, you've had one person by your side: you.

We're taught that it's polite to put others first, but how can you expect any external friendship to last if you don't have a strong bond with yourself first? In this chapter, we're giving you permission to put your relationship with yourself first. It's time to learn how to be your own best friend.

A note from Al

My personal experience of learning to love myself felt like I was a snake shedding its skin. Over and over and over again.

For years I struggled to find my people because I was being the friend I thought people wanted, instead of being my genuine self. I didn't truly know who I was. Instead, I was a shapeshifting chameleon trying to be what I thought others wanted.

When I was in my late teens and early twenties I thought if I was alone, I was a loser and a loner. That if I didn't spend the entire weekend with friends I was some sort of failure.

My biggest fear was being alone on a Friday night. I would quite literally cry, drive home and hang out with my mum just to avoid spending time on my own. I would temporarily delete the social media apps on my phone because seeing everyone else out and about made me feel so sad I felt sick.

Why wasn't that me?

Was there something wrong with me?

All the things my high school bullies said to me felt true. They weren't—but back then it felt like what they said was the truth.

When people at work would ask me, 'So, any weekend plans?' the amount of shame I felt was honestly ridiculous. Sometimes I would make something up so people didn't look down on me, pity me or (my absolute worst fear at the time) think I was a loser. The idea of not having a hectic social life and being at home on a Friday night felt like the worst thing in the world. Like if I was on a TV show I'd be cast as the outcast, hermit or weirdo who couldn't make friends. When I look back at that time now it makes me feel sad for the past me.

When we transition from being teenagers to young adults we're thrust into a world of independence that I'm quite certain none of us are actually ready for. No longer do we see our high school friends five days a week as a way to tick our social interaction box. We have to start building the foundations of our future life, and that is scary as fuck. From moving out of home to starting a new career, growing up is filled with a lot of new territories that can have us spending a lot of time alone.

However, there is one thing we need to realise: *spending time alone is not a failure but a privilege.*

Learning to enjoy my own company came from understanding the difference between being alone and being lonely. Believing that loneliness and being alone is the same thing is a common misconception.

Being alone is physical. It's a fact: in that moment there are no others around you.

Being lonely is a state of mind. It's a feeling. Often this is what fuels our fear of being physically alone. We believe that if there is no one around us we're abandoned and isolated, and it scares the shit out of us—at least, it scared the shit out of me.

One of the most detrimental outcomes of having a deep-seated fear of being alone is that we allow shit situations to seep into our lives. When we're so extremely scared of being alone we end up putting up with harmful situations, jobs, relationships and friends because the alternative—being on our own—feels so paralysing and frightening. We end up plastering our lives with toxic bandaids that seep into other potentially more positive relationships we could be forming. And that's exactly what happened to me. I put up with friends who put me down and an ex-partner who gave the bare minimum.

The more I began prioritising quality time with myself, the more I understood who I was. I learned that I enjoyed little things such as walking to my local cafe for an iced latte, reading fantasy romance novels, buying fresh flowers, ordering from my favourite Italian restaurant and choosing what movie I wanted to watch that night. I liked being empowered to choose what made me happy each day.

It also illuminated the big picture—the things I'd avoided thinking about, such as how I didn't always like the way my friends spoke to me, or that my boyfriend maybe shouldn't have bailed on picking me up from the airport. It made me think about the goals, achievements and experiences that I wanted to go after in life, such as travelling, starting my own company and moving into a new apartment.

After this revelation, within a month (!) I'd ceased contact with my toxic friends, been dumped by my ex and moved into a new house with a random girl from a share house website. She went on to become one of the best things and friends to ever happen to me.

In the space of a month, the vast majority of people I thought I was supposed to love and were supposed to love me back were gone. I was on my own. That month felt like the hardest, most challenging time in my life, but it turned out to be the most valuable. I remember thinking, 'Why is this happening?' But now, when I look back on it, I smile with relief and pride and think, 'I'm so fucking thankful that happened.'

Out of anyone I can spend time with, my number one is myself. There is so much power in enjoying your own time and making decisions with yourself at the centre. The day you realise you can do whatever you want is the day you will find gratitude in every single decision you get to make.

In an episode of his podcast *The Curiosity Chronicle*, Sahil Bloom talks listeners through the American Time Use Survey, which shows that the time we spend alone steadily increases throughout our lives. Bloom implores us to learn to embrace solitude, and to flex our boredom muscle regularly. My take is that we need to find happiness and joy in the time we have to ourselves—there will be a whole lot more of it as we get older. When we have a great relationship with ourselves, great friendships will follow. That's when we know we've got it figured out.

It's not always easy. Sometimes in the moment you won't be the nicest friend to yourself. You will talk to yourself in a way that you'd never speak to someone you love. Voices in your head will tell you you're not good enough, too loud or even sometimes unlikeable.

When you do feel like you are on your own I want you to know that it's okay to not like yourself sometimes, but it's more than okay to love yourself most of the time, too. I want you to sit in the sun and recharge your soul. I want you to start to love the sound of your own laugh. I want you to talk to yourself and make weird noises when you're on your own. I want you to be silly. I want you to realise the radiance you have inside you and how it radiates to the people around you. I want you to learn which small daily treats, such as a morning coffee, bring you joy. I want you to sit on your couch with delicious takeaway and press play on your favourite TV show (my personal favourite is *The Vampire Diaries*).

I hope you realise you are deserving of all the love you've ever received and is yet to come your way.

When the most fulfilling and gratifying relationship you have is with yourself, all the other relationships, friendships and connections in your life further enrich your happiness.

The inbox zero technique

After listening to an episode from the *Do You F*cking Mind Podcast* by Alexis Fernandez, we discovered the inbox zero technique. It changed our lives!

In order to become your own best friend and allow others into your life in a healthy way, you need to come face to face with the thoughts rolling around in your mind. Because we likely all know that friend (or maybe you are that friend) who starts trauma dumping everything that's going wrong with their life whenever they have a few drinks. That's because their mental inbox has been left unchecked.

In the episode 'Self Love—Being Alone vs. Being Lonely', Alexis challenged listeners to ask themselves, when was the last time you spent time alone with your own mind without being pacified by a TV show, scrolling on your phone or listening to a podcast?

Spending time alone with your thoughts sounds scary. Many of us struggle with it, because the noise in our heads becomes loud and we get distracted easily. How often do you sit to watch TV only to pick up your phone and scroll on that, too?

Naval Ravikant is an entrepreneur, investor and modern meditation guru. Before you panic that we're about to go down a woo-woo hole, bear with us. In its simplest sense, meditation is a way to actively spend time alone without being pacified by tools of entertainment. Ravikant sees meditation as a time of self-examination, sitting there with your thoughts and 'the art of doing nothing'.

According to Ravikant, the goal is to reach inbox zero. He encourages us to think of our mind as an email inbox, which if left unchecked will be overflowing with a mix of information, spam, junk and trash. When we spend time alone, unpacified by distraction, we can filter through our mental inbox with the goal to reach inbox zero. Here's how it's done.

Step 1: Sit for at least 60 minutes first thing in the morning

This may feel like a lot of time, but according to Ravikant it takes 30 to 40 minutes to get past the initial noise and chattering filling our heads. Starting in the morning when you're fresh and alert with a clear mind will make this practice easier.

Step 2: Let whatever happens, happen

Often we think of meditation as a regulated, focused practice. But with this theory, you let your mind do whatever it wants to do. According to Ravikant, 'If it wants to talk, you let it talk.

If it wants to fight, you let it fight. If it wants to be quiet, you let it be quiet.' Use this time to think about the things you want to address with yourself.

Step 3: Repeat for 60 days

After doing this exercise for 60 days, most people are able to clear out their mental inbox and the whirlwind that goes on in there. You'll have realisations about things you care about, epiphanies about things that are not worth your time and, most of all, you'll realise the value in spending time on your own, getting to know yourself better. However, we know that life gets busy and spending an hour a day meditating is a bit like 'in what world, babe?'. We get it, we hear you. Even just the simple act of creating a personal ritual, which we go into below, will completely change your mood on a day-to-day basis.

Know your own mind for better friendships

When you're on your own side, you'll start approaching life with a much lighter and more objective outlook. Things that would have annoyed you in the past seem harmless, because you know your values and the opinions, behaviour and thoughts of others start to hold less weight. When you're comfortable in your own company and actually like who you are, *your time becomes more valuable.* You see the time you give to friends as precious. You stop wasting time on people who don't deserve it, because why would you prioritise people who make you feel bad when you can spend time with yourself and feel good?

When you genuinely enjoy your own company, this attitude becomes *infectious* to those around you. And, now that you don't have a whirlwind of spam, junk and trash emails swirling around in your head, you have the energy and clarity to enjoy yourself and give more to your friendships. You'll avoid bringing baggage into friendships and trauma dumping on the people you care about most. Of course, friends are going to be there when times are tough because life isn't always peachy. However, if you're bringing negative vibes to a friendship constantly, that's only going to create a negative friendship.

You will also have the mental space to better support those around you. You've dealt with your own shit so when a good friend needs to lean on you, it's not draining your own mental energy to be there for them. You won't be that friend who always needs to trump others' misfortune. Ever told a friend how hard your break-up was, only to hear that theirs was harder? Or vented to a friend about how work has been super tiring lately, when they say theirs has been *exhausting*?

A lot of the time people don't even realise they're emotional trumping because their mental and emotional inbox has completely run away from them. When you're spending time with yourself and actively aiming to lighten your load you'll also have the capacity to lighten the people around you. You'll have the space to actively listen, understand and respond.

Try this for 60 days and watch yourself become a better friend to yourself and others. We dare you.

Create personal rituals

If the thought of actively spending time alone immediately fills you with fear, don't panic. We have a simple hack for that: creating personal rituals.

Sal, for example, has an extensive evening routine that consists mostly of skincare and listening to Harry Potter audiobooks. Al's evening ritual involves opening up one of her comfort fantasy books that she's read about seven times already.

Everyone's personal rituals look completely different, but that's the point. They're personal. They're something that only you can do on your own. It's your time to recharge and refuel the jet so you can take off when you need to. Spending time on these rituals puts gas back in your tank, giving you more energy for your connections. (You know those moments when you're talking to a friend and you can *feel* your eyes glazing over but you just can't help it? Yeah, you're running on empty, bestie.)

There's a good chance you already have your own personal rituals without even knowing it. It could be listening to your favourite podcast (we heard *Two Broke Chicks* is really good) or going for a hot girl walk on a Sunday morning. Think about that thing you do to be with yourself, and actively be present rather than just passing the time in between social interactions.

What's self-love got to do with it?

Sometimes our inability to be our own best friend stems from a lack of self-love.

Your feelings towards yourself don't exist in a vacuum. They ooze their way into the other relationships in your love life, workplace and, of course, friendships. It's when you're feeling insecure about yourself that you'll project by throwing snarky comments at your friends. It's when honest conversations are replaced by passive-aggressive remarks. It's when you'll see your friends' wins in life as competition instead of accomplishments to admire.

All of these things will slowly but surely eat away at even the strongest of friendships, and can't be resolved until you've truly learned to love and live with yourself. But, like we said, learning to love yourself is like training a muscle. You have to nurture and feed this muscle for it to become stronger and support you.

Loving yourself is having a genuine appreciation of yourself. It means putting yourself first and not sacrificing who you are for other people. Remember, if they're true friends, they would never want this from you anyway.

When you genuinely love yourself it means you'll never settle for a single thing that's less than you deserve.

Most importantly, loving yourself is knowing that you're not perfect. Far from it, actually. It's knowing exactly who you are, warts and all, and still thinking you're the bomb diggity because your positives outweigh your negatives.

We can promise you, absolutely no one thinks in their head, 'Wow, I'm perfect'—unless they live in a state of delusion and, if so, they're probably a bit of a narcissist. Even your idols and major celebrities like Kim Kardashian have moments of imposter syndrome and self-doubt.

It wasn't until our mid-twenties that we both stepped into the skins we not only felt comfortable in, but genuinely liked. It's an ongoing journey, and sometimes we like ourselves more than other times. However, once we made self-love a priority we found that meeting people and making friends became easier than ever. We didn't feel the need to over-analyse everything we said before we said it, or fall into an anxious spiral if people didn't ask to hang out with us. As icon, drag queen and our reality TV mummy RuPaul says, 'If you can't love yourself, how the hell are you going to love anybody else?'

A note from Sal

For a long time, I felt like I was the ugly friend. No need to cue the violins: I'm not fishing for compliments or kicking off the Sally Sob Story here. It's simply a pattern I noticed pretty early on in life, probably because my older sister slash biological other half Meg has always been drop-dead gorgeous. I don't hold any resentment towards her because of this. It's not her choice, and her outer beauty is just one of many amazing qualities about her. From my early life, people regularly spoke of Meg's beauty and said they couldn't believe I was her little sister. This set me up with a bit of an unhealthy mindset around comparing myself to others.

And it's not just Meg. I can't count how many times guys have come up to me only to say, 'Your friend is really hot. Is she single?' Guys have literally slid into my DMs to ask my friends out through me. It grated on me, but I also knew I was my own worst critic and reminded myself that surely no one else thought of me as the ugly friend. It was all in my head, right?

This was until many years ago at a friend's work farewell drinks. This friend is one of my closest gal pals whom I've known since I was a kid. She is one of those people who can light up a room, and I've always admired her for that. At the party, she was walking back from the bar, looking fabulous as usual and turning heads as she went. As she walked towards me, though, one of her friends turned to me and said, 'Oh, that must suck for you.'

At that time I was in my mid-twenties, had been in a loving relationship for over ten years, was at a good point in my career and felt pretty proud of the person I'd grown up to be. I certainly wasn't looking for attention from randoms in a bar (and neither was my friend, to be honest). Yet that one remark from a complete stranger (whom I never saw again, mind you) was like a slap in the face. It immediately took me back to that feeling of being the ugly friend.

It shook me. For weeks following, I found myself retreating into old patterns. I'd constantly compare myself to my friends. When they were feeling their fantasy and looking hot as fuck on a night out, the little voice in the back of my head would start picking apart all of the things I didn't like about my appearance. I wouldn't want to get in group photos. I was even starting to turn down invites because I didn't want to face the meltdown over what to wear. While I never verbally communicated it, I could feel my insecurities starting to seep into my relationships.

I had been down this spiral before and it wasn't a trip I was keen to take again. This problem wasn't going to fix itself. I knew that being showered in compliments by my friends, boyfriend or some random stranger in a bar wasn't the answer. That's because it was never about anyone else. It was always about me. (Cue the inspirational montage.)

I started being kinder to myself. As negative thoughts popped into my head, I'd swat them away with compliments to myself. I started going to the gym regularly, focusing on exercise I actually enjoyed and how it made me feel, not how it made me look. I prioritised my health and happiness over my vanity. I put less stock on compliments I received about my physical appearance, placing greater value on feedback about my personality, career or skills. You know, the stuff that actually matters?!

A few months went by, and then one night, it hit me. I was on the dance floor at that same bar where my friend held her farewell, and it was like the world slowed down. I looked around and saw my best friends singing and dancing along with me in reckless abandon. They didn't care how I looked or what other people thought of me. They didn't need me to be the successful friend or the smart friend or the hot friend. Their friendship with me wasn't predicated on some weird agenda. It was my sense of humour, the fun memories we shared and my impeccable taste in music (probably, I'm just assuming here) that they loved about me. It was from that moment I started letting go of the bullshit and finally saw myself as my friends did.

Ditch the negative self-talk

The way we speak to ourselves matters. So often we talk to ourselves in a way that we would never speak to our friends.

We humans often fall into the nasty habit of holding ourselves to a higher standard than we do everyone else. Our internal monologue expects so much and sets completely unachievable goals. Then, as soon as we inevitably don't meet them, we turn into our own harshest critic, a personal Simon Cowell, an inner saboteur.

The list of daily activities we believe we are 'supposed' to achieve is overwhelming. In a simple 24-hour day we expect ourselves to work our 'dream job', drink two litres of water, do our washing, call our parents, catch up with friends, move our bodies, cook and eat a nutritious meal and the list goes on. Even if you're a superhero, that's simply not achievable. Yet we continue to expect it of ourselves and be unkind inwardly when we fail to meet these standards.

It's clear we need to cut ourselves some slack, but expecting that we will never again talk negatively to ourselves is setting ourselves up for failure, too. It is important to allow ourselves a controlled space of constructive criticism but to rein it in as soon as it turns into self-sabotage.

Jay Shetty, popular podcast host and author of the book *Think Like a Monk*, eloquently illuminates why it is so simple to fall into negative self-talk: 'Focusing on something negative is something that we feel, whereas when we read something positive, it's something that we think.' He says it's easier to get swept up in negative self-talk because we feel negative emotions much more strongly than positive ones. It takes more work to feel something positive on an emotional level rather than just thinking it.

Being kind to ourselves is something we need to learn. It's also about controlling the environments we're in and creating positive surroundings. If you're working a job that causes you to feel a blanket of heaviness every time you clock on, if you scroll through a social media feed full of people who make you feel bad about yourself, or if you spend your time with people who weigh you down rather than lightening your load, of course you're going to be feeling low. A key to ditching negative self-talk is creating an environment of self-kindness.

Identify your boundaries and stick to them

We can likely all think of a situation in which we've said yes when we really wanted to say no. How many times have you thought that if you say yes, maybe someone will like you more? We try to avoid tension, pressure or disappointing someone by saying yes when, in reality, our internal monologue is dramatically screaming, 'No, stop. Please, no!' as the claws of obligation drag us away from our warm, soft bed.

First off, this is completely and utterly human. We all have a deep-rooted human desire to be liked. This can sometimes cause us to go against a want or need for ourselves, where we sacrifice a natural and normal boundary. Then we fall into the quicksand of beating ourselves up about how we regret saying yes. 'Why couldn't I just stand up for myself?' We begin directing our frustration inward.

Many of us find setting boundaries difficult because there is a misalignment between who we are, what we want and what we need. Sure, you may not *want* to pick up heavy boxes while helping your friend move house, but you like being there for your friends. You do not *need* to go out for Friday drinks when you're feeling bone tired and yearning for some time to yourself, but you have a fear of missing out or don't want to be perceived as antisocial.

If you're not respecting your own needs and setting boundaries accordingly, this will spill over into your relationships. When you're begrudgingly in your Uber on your way to happy hour drinks, you're not going to show up as your best self. As a result, you'll be a lacking companion to your mates.

The beautiful thing about boundaries is that they're not only a healthy practice for you, but they also act like weed killer for your friendship garden. A good friend will never be upset with you for saying no, nor will they make you feel uncomfortable for doing so. If you find yourself being scared to tell a friend no because they've reacted poorly to you setting boundaries in the past, that means it's time to rethink that friendship.

It is important to note that it takes two to tango—both parties need to respect each other's boundaries for it to work. You also need to stay firm, and avoid breaking your own boundaries. If you've got a rubber arm and allow your friend to encourage and cajole you into doing something you don't want to, such as going to Friday beveraginos, you've just shown that person *and* yourself you don't respect your own boundaries. And if *you* don't respect your own boundaries, how will others know to respect them?

A note from Al

The biggest detriment to setting boundaries is when we expect the other person to have an X-Men–like telepathic ability to know what we're thinking.

My childhood best friend, Bonnie, got a boyfriend and we went from a duo to a trio. While I would still see her, her boyfriend, Jeremy, was never too far behind. I didn't always care about this, because I *did* like him and we'd still have fun. However, the trio dynamic was never the same as when it was just me and Bonnie spending quality time together. Sometimes I didn't even know Jeremy was coming and *poof* he'd show up. I missed one-on-one time with my friend, but I feared that if it couldn't be the three of us it would be nothing at all. I didn't want to lose my friendship with Bonnie.

I didn't realise this at the time, but by not stating my needs I was continuously crossing my own boundary. I was expecting Bonnie to telepathically read my mind that I wanted more time with her one-on-one. Sure, it would've been nice for her to also want that, but again, this isn't X-Men.

One day I'd finally grown the courage to send a text and say, 'Do you mind if we hang out just you and me today? I miss our girl time.' It didn't need to be a long-winded message or a major confrontation. I just needed to set the boundary, and respect it.

Bonnie didn't even bat an eyelid at the question. In fact, she apologised, saying it had only just dawned on her how long it had been since we'd had some quality time.

Even though it was a bit nerve-racking, being honest with my friend stopped a seed of resentment growing. I didn't let the issue bubble to the point of it blowing up and us having a friendship fallout. Six months later, when Bonnie and her boyfriend broke up, I was even more relieved I had set those clear boundaries and held on to this friendship that would last the distance.

Of course setting boundaries can be hard, but I promise you, the right friendships are all the more healthy for it.

If you're new to setting boundaries, you may be asking yourself 'How do I get started?' We're so glad you asked.

What boundaries do you want to set?

Reflect on your past and current friendships. What were some of the boundaries that were continuously crossed (including by yourself)? Perhaps you found yourself frustrated at a friend who was constantly asking for favours without giving any in return. Or maybe you began dreading social engagements you would usually be excited by because your social battery had officially carked it. Saying no to your friends is one of the hardest boundaries to learn but absolutely fundamental to healthy relationships. We should be saying no as much as we're saying yes, in our opinion. Balance, baby.

Clarify and articulate to yourself what your boundary is

Once you've identified the boundary you want to set, get clear on what that boundary is and why it's important to you. There is always a reason as to why you're setting a boundary. Understanding this yourself sets a strong foundation for consistency.

Let's say you're feeling stressed about finances and you're not wanting to spend $90 on bottomless margs for a friend's birthday. That's obviously fair enough, and an important boundary to set. You shouldn't be putting yourself into debt for your friends.

Learn how to express boundaries

Don't communicate boundaries defensively; it makes others feel like they need to be on the offensive. Communicate your boundaries respectfully but firmly.

Articulating to your friend that you don't want to spend $90 on their birthday drinks, and doing so as soon as possible, gives them notice and shows respect for their plans, too. It is as simple as messaging the birthday boy/girl/human one-on-one saying:

Thank you so much for the invitation, however I'm currently saving money and have to put funds towards X. Would you like to come over one night this week and I can make us dinner to celebrate your birthday?

Hold firm to your boundary

You may get a few friends trying to push your boundary. They might put the pressure on: 'Why aren't you coming?!' or 'But $90 is actually really cheap for bottomless margs!'

This doesn't mean you need to jump on the defence, but you do need to remain firm in the boundary you set. Remind people that you *do* want to spend time with them, that in an ideal world you'd be attending, and there is always next time. At the end of the day, it's not a big deal.

Respect others' boundaries

Take note of when your friends are setting boundaries with you, and respect them if you can. If you can't come up with a recent example, this may be a lesson to be a bit more conscious—because we can promise you, your friends have definitely tried to set boundaries with you.

Whenever a friend is saying no, asking for something to be different or potentially needing some space, do not push them. There is a difference between being encouraging and being disrespectful of someone's boundaries.

When a friend is setting a boundary always thank them and acknowledge it with action. Words are great, but action is change.

Practise self-compassion (or not giving a damn)

Florence Given, an author, podcast host and all-round bad-arse, says that her path to self-compassion began when she was fourteen years old and gave herself three minutes to not give a damn. As she lay in a park surrounded by girls from her school, she told herself she could choose one song to play without caring what anyone thought.

For three minutes (give or take, we're guessing), she was able to unshackle herself from the weight of other people's perceptions and, more importantly, be herself and not care.

The weight of expectations we put on ourselves is already overwhelming. Carrying the weight of every single other person in the world's expectations is paralysing.

We'd like to pose a question to ask yourself. Do you not like something about yourself because *you* don't like it, or because you think others won't?

Breaking the mould of living for others is not only freeing but liberating. Deciding you don't care if people don't like you or the weird little things you enjoy is empowering, and also enthralling.

Both of us love to express our creativity through fashion. We love band tees linking us to our favourite fandoms (One Direction anyone?) and colourful cowboy boots. Recently Al is absolutely frothing over wearing ribbons in her hair because it makes her feel like a 'pretty little ladybug'.

Wear what you want, post what you want on social media, shave your head if you bloody well feel like it. At the end of the day, we are little specks in the universe and it's not that deep, so we might as well enjoy ourselves. When you don't give a damn, you embody confidence. You become infectious to those around you—someone others enjoy being around, *and* you'll enjoy being around yourself, too.

It's naive to go through life with the expectation that everyone will like you. It's a tough pill to swallow, but you won't always be everyone's cup of tea.

Imagine what you could do if you repurposed all the energy you spend overthinking and caring about what other people think?

Learn how to self-reflect and be honest with yourself

Self-reflection can be a bittersweet skill to master, but it's essential for any great relationship. It's not an opportunity to beat yourself up about the time you fumbled your words trying to order a morning coffee or when you sent a work email to the wrong person. It's a practice of objectively assessing your strengths and weaknesses; of rewarding yourself with pride for moments you feel good about, and learning from things you think you could improve upon.

It takes a lot for someone to be able to acknowledge when they've messed up, but it also makes them an even better friend. Owning up to things we could improve in our behaviour creates a positive environment that will encourage others to do the same.

Imagine if you're constantly doubling down and never admitting fault in a situation. There is a high chance the people in your life are going to follow suit. But if everyone is self-reflecting, this creates a healthy friendship ecosystem where everyone is owning up to their stuff. Sometimes it may even be your friends encouraging you to self-reflect—for example, when they notice you're talking to your ex, who is most definitely not the best influence, again.

The best part about self-reflection is it allows you to spin your negative thoughts and insecurities into a positive change. It's not only going to build a better relationship inward, but outward, too.

If you're constantly waking up after nights out with absolutely crippling hangxiety, it might be time to reflect a little and ask yourself what there is to be anxious about. Dancing on a table? Slay. That sounds fun. Getting a bit narky at your mate after a few shots? Probably good to understand why that happened and also be okay with apologising.

Putting ourselves in the hot seat is no easy task. Here are some questions to ask yourself to prompt your personal performance review:

- ⊛ What's on my mind?
- ⊛ What has made me happy recently?
- ⊛ How can I experience that more in my life?
- ⊛ What has made me feel down recently?
- ⊛ What can I do to avoid that feeling?
- ⊛ Most importantly, Al's personal favourite: am I just hungry?

Stop comparing yourself

We know, it's easy for us to say 'stop comparing yourself' and hard to put this into action!

Our society is built on a backbone of comparison to become better. We see women especially suffering from this. The fact that women are constantly pitted against each other in the media as competition instead of colleagues yet we rarely see this treatment for their male counterparts? Fucking bonkers.

When we're taught to compare ourselves to the models on Instagram or the latest Kardashian campaign, it becomes a natural toxic habit in our everyday lives, too. Whether we're comparing ourselves to our partner's ex, our co-workers or, yes, even our friends, the green-eyed monster has no mercy and takes no prisoners.

Jealousy is poison to friendships. And when we're constantly focusing on everything others have, we don't practise gratitude for the things we have or the amazing qualities we bring to our own and others' lives.

It's important to note that it's okay to want something for yourself that you see in your friends. For years, Al would look at Sal's romantic partnership and think how lovely it would be to be in such a healthy relationship. Did it make her feel bitterness towards Sal for finding her soulmate? Absolutely not. Recently Sal's partner asked Al if she found their PDA annoying. Al responded, 'Why would I find it annoying that my best friend is receiving the love she deserves? I want that for her!' It's okay to want something for yourself and be happy for the person who has that thing, too. Al was able to recognise the good in her own situation. The three years she was single in her twenties were absolutely amazing and allowed her to foster a relationship with herself that prepared her to enter a healthy romantic relationship later on in life.

It's naive to think that you'll wake up one day with the sun shining and the birds chirping and never compare yourself to anyone ever again. But here's your homework. Next time you compare yourself to someone else, think of three qualities you absolutely froth about yourself. Bonus points for writing them on your mirror so you never, ever forget them.

Romanticise your life

This is your reminder that you are the main character of the movie that is your life. We always look back on years gone by—the 'golden years' of the past. When we're reflecting on life's highlights we usually think of the milestone moments: graduations, landing a dream job, taking our first big overseas trip.

But what about the small joys that make up everyday life? When you wake up on a weekend thinking it's a workday, but then you realise you can sleep in. That first sip of a really crispy glass of Coca-Cola when you're severely hungover. When a banger you totally forgot about pops up on a Spotify playlist. It's these small and seemingly insignificant moments that we can enjoy in solitude and should gaze upon with rose-coloured glasses.

Make more time to do things for yourself and by yourself, and actually take in how it makes you feel. The list of ways you can romanticise your life is almost endless, but let's start off with something as simple as your Sunday morning routine.

Put on an outfit that makes you feel happy. It could be your cutest coordinated activewear set, a Pinterest-worthy sundress or oversized sweats and a t-shirt à la Adam Sandler. Pack a book or queue up a podcast and find a cosy seat at your favourite cafe. Treat yourself to a delicious breakfast and your coffee order of choice. Don't rush. Really indulge in every sip and bite. Then, spend the rest of the day ticking off some of your favourite activities. Put some of your old clothes up on Depop, watch some YouTube or buy some fresh fruit from the farmers' market. Whatever you want. Because that's the point: you're doing exactly what you want and soaking in every second of it.

You're not doing these things alone because you don't have anyone to hang out with. You're doing them alone because you *want* to. By slowing down and romanticising everyday life, you can really enjoy the good old days while they're happening. You'll still draw joy from spending time with your friends, but it means you won't be reliant on anyone else to find sources of happiness in everyday life.

Being your own best friend isn't pathetic, it's powerful. There's so much magic to be found in enjoying time alone. You just have to give yourself permission to do it.

• •

Checklist: 40 solo activities to do on your own

- ❑ Draw yourself a bath.
- ❑ Go for a hike.
- ❑ Read a new book (maybe it's this one *wink*).
- ❑ Talk to yourself.
- ❑ Make a to-do list and check things off it.
- ❑ Do a hair mask.
- ❑ Head to a museum or art exhibition.

- ❑ Get your nails done or paint your own nails.
- ❑ Follow a yoga video on YouTube.
- ❑ Sit in the sun.
- ❑ Meditate.
- ❑ Have a picnic.
- ❑ Make a new music playlist.
- ❑ Get a massage.
- ❑ Try cooking a new recipe.
- ❑ Move your body.
- ❑ Try at-home pottery.
- ❑ Buy yourself some fresh flowers.
- ❑ Try a new look. Make-up, hairstyle or whatever you like!
- ❑ Sign up for an online class (time to learn French maybe?).
- ❑ Volunteer.
- ❑ Go to a new gym class.
- ❑ Explore the markets.
- ❑ Make a wish list from your favourite shopping site.
- ❑ Make some new Pinterest boards.
- ❑ Try a new coffee shop.
- ❑ Browse op shops and antique stores.
- ❑ Order your favourite takeaway meal.
- ❑ Start a DIY project.
- ❑ Go to a comedy bar.
- ❑ Update your résumé.
- ❑ Listen to a podcast or audiobook.
- ❑ Splurge on something for yourself.
- ❑ Deep clean your room.
- ❑ Watch a sunrise or sunset.
- ❑ Do a paint and sip class.

- [ ] Spend an afternoon at the library.
- [ ] See a gig.
- [ ] Journal.
- [ ] Last but not least, open up your bedside drawer and practise some self-love. You know exactly what we mean.

• •

A REASON,
A SEASON'
OR A LIFETIME

Our podcast *Two Broke Chicks* is all about life lessons in your twenties and beyond. From relationships and careers to self-love and mental health, we've covered a lot of the big kahuna life lessons we face as we enter adulthood.

When we're doing research ahead of a podcast recording, we often invite our Instagram audience to share the life lessons they've picked up along the way. Not only is it amazing to hand the microphone over to our chicks, but we also love hearing stories, hot takes and honest perspectives from people outside of our immediate circle. Many of these gems of wisdom from our chicks are sprinkled throughout the book.

Friendship is one of the topics that garners the juiciest responses. In season four, we did an episode on life lessons about friendship and the responses varied from validating and illuminating to heartbreaking, hilarious and genuinely shocking. Some of you need to dump your friends immediately. Anyway, moving on.

Overwhelmingly, the most common life lesson our chicks shared was, 'People come into your life for a reason, a season or a lifetime.' It's actually the opening line and title of a poem attributed to Brian A. 'Drew' Chalker. It has become a popular quote that we've shared many times on the podcast. However, we were still a little surprised by how many people in our audience either resonated with that phrase or came across that life lesson through their own experiences with friendship.

For many of us, having a BFF was lorded as *the* most important piece of social currency throughout primary and high school. There was a social hierarchy with friends at the bottom, best friends one rung up and BFFs at the top. The emphasis being on that last F: *forever.* We grow up believing that our friends will stick with us forever. But, as we covered in Chapter 1, the only friendship you can count on with this level of permanency is the one you have with yourself.

The idea that we should have a core group of forever friends akin to a 1990s TV sitcom is so heavily ingrained in us. Perhaps that's why it's such a rude shock when we get older and learn that friendships rarely do last forever. Even as two fully grown women who truly believe that friends come into our lives for a reason, a season or a lifetime, we still struggle with this. It's hard not to look back on friendships lost and not feel like a failure.

As life propels us into different eras, it's also common to forge close bonds with different types of people. It's pretty normal for people to make friendships in different areas of their lives—to go to someone's birthday party or wedding and find a mixed bag of friends from school, mates from uni, colleagues and teammates from their mixed sport team. As we and our lives change, so do our relationships.

A lot of the time, friendships flourish out of forced proximity and, once that common tie is cut, they're difficult to maintain. We're sure many of you can relate to the experience of losing touch with your old uni mates. Maybe you started a new job and no longer keep in touch with the work wife who used to get a play-by-play of your life over coffee every morning. You're not alone if you just got a pang of guilt being reminded that you really need to reach out to that one friend you haven't spoken to in a long time.

It's important to recognise that some friendships come into our lives and, like the seasons, they pass. Just because you've grown distant from someone you were once super close with doesn't mean you'll never reconnect. Some friendships ebb and flow, coming in and out of your life periodically. On the other hand, some friendships do only last for a finite amount of time. While it's totally normal to feel nostalgic or sad about a friendship that isn't as present in your life as it once was, it's also an important part of life to reconcile. We'll talk through exactly how to do this and why you should embrace it instead of fearing it later in this chapter. Then there are the friendships that make you look back and wonder, 'What the fuck was I thinking?' The ones that burn bright and fast and collapse in on themselves.

In this chapter, we're going to break down the different types and seasons of friendship you may encounter in life. First, let's break down each part of Chalker's infamous quote and how it materialises in our friendships.

A reason

TL;DR A reason friendship has a start and sometimes an end, and it often leaves you with a lesson learned. These relationships spark a realisation or benefit you in some way—whether you knew you needed it or not. These friendships come into your life for a reason and you walk away knowing yourself better, whether it's learned the easy way or the hard way.

It's our mantra that every experience, relationship, bad day and good day gifts us a life lesson. Naturally, this includes friendships. Whether it's the person you bonded with in the club bathroom for five minutes, your best friend from preschool whom you haven't seen in decades or a friendship that turned sour, you cross paths with specific people for particular reasons.

Even the most toxic of friendships can teach us something. Think back to a friendship that ended badly. Perhaps you learned what you do and don't want out of a friendship. Maybe you learned that you're a bit of a people pleaser and it inspired you to practise saying no. The friendship might have made you more resilient or helped you pick up red flags that you now avoid. Or maybe you didn't put as much effort into your friendship as you should've and it taught you not to take relationships for granted. If the friendship is over but you wish it didn't end, maybe it taught you about conflict resolution and what you could do to save a friendship in future. Whatever transpired, it's likely that you're a better person and friend because of it.

This isn't a message of toxic positivity, though. We're not saying that these reasons are always blessings. Nor are we saying that you should feel grateful when you've had a friend who treats you like shit because there's a 'life lesson' buried somewhere deep in there. You're allowed to look back on a dumpster fire of a friendship and label it as such. Sadly we can't jump in a time machine and reverse any of the not-so-nice friendships we've experienced. With some perspective, plus time to heal and process, we may as well use it as an opportunity to learn something about ourselves and how we want to live our lives. Life is too short to have bad friends.

A friendship break-up is a unique kind of heartache and it hurts like a bitch. In our experience, reflecting on what you learned from that friendship can help you mourn that person, let go of the pain and start healing. It can help you put a full stop on that chapter of your life and turn the page to enter a new one.

A note from Sal

When I was around nine years old, my best friend and I had a falling-out with another friend in our class. When we recounted the blow-up to my mum, she suggested that we write our ex-friend a letter explaining how we had been hurt and what we'd learned from the conflict. But instead of sending the old friend the letter, Mum suggested that we take it down to the local creek, burn it and wash the remains away. (I don't know how responsible or environmentally friendly it is to encourage a tween to burn a letter and wash it down a creek, but alas it was advice given with good intention.) We'd all probably been watching way too much *Charmed*, but it worked. My friend and I both felt incredibly empowered and freed from the toxic friendship we'd previously felt weighed down by.

Many times since then, I've used this technique of writing things down on paper and disposing of it as a way to move on from past trauma or relationships. There's not always fire involved but I've found the symbolic gesture of writing something down and then destroying it a powerful way to let go of something from the past. It also gives you a really intentional opportunity to reflect on how you're feeling and what you've learned from the experience. I 10/10 recommend.

A reason friendship doesn't always have to be a bad situation with a silver lining. Sometimes it can be an incredibly positive and life-changing experience that has had a huge impact on the person you are today.

A note from Al

One of my reason friendships was the spark behind my sexuality epiphany.

For my entire life to that point I had thought of myself as straight. I'd only ever kissed boys, had crushes on boys and dated boys. I'd pictured myself marrying a man. A lot of this was due to my upbringing. I don't think I met a single out-and-proud person from the LGBTQIA+ community until my twenties. As a kid the only thing I knew was that purple and green were 'lesbian colours'— obviously not true, but kids are stupid. The only exposure I had to the community was Dame Edna on *Sunrise* and the over-dramatised same-sex relationships on television shows such as *Glee*. During high school, all of my friends were in heterosexual relationships, dreaming of weddings, buying houses and having kids.

I remember a crucial moment with my first boyfriend when he turned to me and asked, 'Aren't you excited to be together forever?'

Cue immediate panic.

Because I wasn't. Like, at all.

This wasn't to fault him, but I had so much more to experience and learn. I wanted to go and explore and live, and while people can still do that in relationships, I knew this was not that kind of relationship. I felt like a wild horse being led into a pony shed.

We broke up and I moved away to a different part of Sydney. During this time I met Sal and so many other incredible creatives and humans that were different to everything I'd experienced growing up. The way these people spoke about sexuality was inclusive. They communicated in a way that showed there was nothing taboo or wrong with being queer. There were no drunk girls saying, 'I could kiss a girl but, like, I just don't think I could have sex with one.' (Side note: please stop saying this. It's homophobic and insulting.)

As I started to become more involved with people who were more free with their sexuality, I felt the tight grip I had on my own reins loosen. I started to question myself. Why had I put my sexuality into a box when, really, it never deserved to be in there? (Just ask my old Barbie dolls who would constantly be left in a scissoring position. Sorry Ken.)

As the reins loosened, my confusion grew. Was I gay? Bisexual? Straight and curious? I had no fucking clue.

I was also scared. I was scared my female friends would no longer feel comfortable around me. I was scared of labelling myself. I was scared that because I liked both guys and girls, neither would like me.

Sometimes I'd be drunk enough that I'd finally be comfortable to voice my confusion and ask Sal what she thought.

'If I like to kiss girls does this make me gay?', or, 'I kinda like girls but I don't know if I'd say I'm bisexual?' And so on and so forth.

When having these conversations, we were always tipsy and I never actually 'came out'.

Until I met Jack.

Jack is one of the most amazing individuals I've met. He is so authentically himself and the most fabulous human. He was one of my roommates' best friends and had recently moved to Sydney. He needed a place to stay while he got set up so moved in with us for a couple of weeks.

I was on leave from work so Jack and I ended up spending a lot of time getting our nails done together, drinking rosé and talking about love, life and stupid stuff that made us laugh. By this point I was calling both girls and guys hot, but in a way that people mightn't have known if it was attraction or admiration.

One afternoon Jack and I were sitting in the sun on the porch of our somewhat hazardously built share house, talking about people we thought were hot. Jack casually said, 'Yeah, but you like girls too, right?' to which I, without thought, replied, 'Yeah.' In that moment, I was so comfortable, so myself that I didn't even fully realise the weight of the question. I'd just answered it honestly.

It was as if someone was asking me about the weather, rather than it being the first time I was telling someone I wasn't straight.

To Jack it didn't matter. It was simply who I am.

As our friendship continued, I blossomed into more confidence with who I am. The first time I kissed a girl, I immediately told Jack. The first time I had sex with a girl, Jack was in our living room innocently watching *Will & Grace* with the volume turned up and I walked out with a grin from ear to ear. He was so happy for me. It made me feel so light. So free.

Because of that friendship, my sexuality was no longer black or white—and I realised that was perfectly okay. I don't know if I'd be where I am today if it wasn't for Jack. I think I'd still be a little confused, if I'm honest.

Jack was the reason I became so comfortable being me. I'm not straight, bi, gay, pan or whatever label people might like to put on themselves. Just let a girl be a horny sheila without having to put herself in a filing cabinet, ffs.

I'm simply Alex. I love people I love, I want to kiss people I want to kiss and I flirt with people I want to flirt with.

That's it and that's all there should be to it.

A season

TL;DR A seasonal friendship is one that is with you during a certain period of your life. It might be a significant period of time that brings you personal evolution, but that eventually ends either temporarily or forever. It might be a friendship that lasts for a specific period of time such as school, a certain job or the time you spend playing in a particular sporting team. It isn't always a big, meaningful part of your life; it could be simply a phase you go through. It may or may not lead to a huge epiphany.

If you look back on your life, you can probably pinpoint the different eras based on the friends you surrounded yourself with at the time. Sometimes friends come and go dramatically, but often the friendship shift is very subtle. Sometimes you don't even realise how much your friendship dynamics have changed until you look back. This realisation can be sucky, but take comfort in knowing it's a pretty universal experience.

A 2009 study by sociologist Gerald Mollenhorst found that most friendships exist in seven-year seasons. Through a survey of over 1000 participants aged 18 to 65, Mollenhorst found that we generally replace half of our friends with new ones every seven years. The study found that while the size of our network stays roughly the same, only 48 per cent of the people in our friendship sphere remain the same with each seven-year period.

At first glance, these statistics may seem kind of harsh. But when you think about it, it definitely lines up with the seasons of life that many of us experience. For example, an Australian high school experience typically lasts for six years. In our case, we both went to university with a couple of our high school friends, so maintaining a handful of those friendships remained pretty effortless for the following year or two. We were still in the habit of inviting our high school friends to birthday parties, even if we weren't catching up with them at the uni bar between classes. However, as time stretched on, many of these friendships fizzled out.

If you look back on the core friendships you had at the end of high school, you might notice that only a handful remain in your life today. The rest may not have ended in dramatic conflict, but kind of just fizzled out. Perhaps you're not close anymore, but still exchange the odd 'Congratulations!' comment on an engagement or baby announcement post. These are seasonal friendships.

A note from Sal

I learned that friendships are seasonal pretty early in life. When I was eight, my parents made what felt like a split-second decision to move us from the Sutherland Shire to the coastal town of Wollongong.

It was only about 60 minutes south of where I had grown up, but it may as well have been a foreign country.

While I was sad to leave my primary school chums, I was *devastated* to leave the group of kids I grew up with in my street. There were four super-close families who lived within a few houses of each other. Each of them had between three to four kids, so naturally we formed our own tiny street gangs. We were like the Lost Boys from Peter Pan, divided into a boys' group (led by my older brother Declan) and a girls' group (made up of my older sister Meg and our three best friends, Sarah and Sian [who were also sisters], and Nikki).

We all lived within 60 seconds of each other, so we spent almost all of our waking hours together. When we weren't at school, we spent our time riding our bikes around the street, making up dances to *So Fresh* CD mixes and building forts. In between that we'd walk in and out of each other's houses to raid pantries or our parents' wallets for spare change to spend on lollies at the corner shop.

Sarah, Sian and Nikki may as well have been our sisters. So when my parents dropped the bomb on us that we were moving, naturally my first thought was, 'But I can't leave my friends!'

We made a pact to remain best friends forever. We vowed to visit each other often and to become pen pals to keep each other updated on our lives. (This was the early 2000s, so it's not like we had social media to stay connected.)

On the day of the big move, me, Meg and our three best friends stood in a circle in our lounge room swaying to the song 'High' by Lighthouse Family. As tears streamed down our little faces, we held each other and belted our hearts out to the chorus that we felt perfectly encapsulated how our friendship was going to bond us forever.

While it is a bona fide nineties *banger*, I still can't listen to that song without tearing up and feeling that same pang of loss—because, spoiler alert: we didn't stay friends forever.

The whole pen pal thing didn't last long, and that 60 minute distance between us as kids was enough to stunt the friendships from growing any further. We did eventually follow each other on social media once Facebook and Instagram came around, but the friendships were already cut short.

While I can only imagine what mischief we would've gotten up to as a bunch of teens, I'm grateful to at least have had those three as my introduction to friendship as a child. I owe so many of my most wholesome and cherished childhood memories to those girls. Yet we've barely spoken over the last 20 years. It made me realise that sometimes friendships are forced to end, but you can still appreciate them for what they were and how they've ultimately helped you become the person you are today.

We've also both experienced seasonal friendships in workplaces. Our friendship with each other was forged when we entered our first full-time jobs. By the time we left that workplace to prioritise *Two Broke Chicks*, Sal had been there for almost eight years and Al was nearing five years. We're not sure if this experience was specific to us, but the workplace felt a little like an extension of high school. It was a tech startup and much of the staff was made up of fresh-faced twenty-somethings who were straight out of uni.

Every morning we'd grab coffee together before we settled into work. We'd spend our lunch breaks going to gym classes together or eating our lunch at cafeteria-style tables in the office.

Like clockwork, at 4 pm on Friday we'd wind down with a couple of bevs in the office and end up plonking ourselves at a local bar to blow off some steam. While the Sal and Al work wife relationship was a revered and unholy union that couldn't be matched, we did also belong to a big group of friends at our workplace. They became *real* friends too. We'd confide in each other about a lot more than work and were there for each other through many milestone moments, from engagements and baby announcements to heartbreaks. We'd mourn each person's absence when they moved on to different roles.

Once The Thing That Shall Not Be Named hit in 2020, the work friend dynamic shifted dramatically. It's probably a familiar story: we went from Friday drinks to Friday trivia nights on Zoom. Our morning coffee catch-ups were replaced by morning conference calls. As any sort of 'novelty' associated with lockdown or working from home wore off, the online catch-ups began to taper off. The Slack notification bell dinged less frequently. Even when we began to return to the office, the vibe had shifted. People were more likely to function in a hybrid work-from-home and office situation, and we struggled to match days in the office and find time to catch up.

While life has returned to relative normalcy, it also feels like we're stuck in the world's longest hangover from the pandemic. Our social batteries are smaller. People are less likely to stick around on a Friday for after-work drinks. Many people are exhausted from spending time in the office and would rather head home, or save their social energy for their 'real friends'.

In early 2023 we moved on from that workplace to take *Two Broke Chicks* solo. We've kept in touch with our old workmates less and less. Again, this timing fits with the seven-year theory.

Seasons of friendship can also change as you enter different eras in your other relationships. If you're in your single era, you may have that one pal who is your go-to wing-person for nights out every weekend without fail. If either of you end up in a relationship, it's likely that quite a few of those weekends will now be occupied by quality time with a partner.

We don't have personal experience of this, but we can also only imagine that friendship dynamics would change dramatically if children enter the equation. You can hardly blame your mate for dropping the ball on your weekly Taco Tuesday tradition if they're taking care of a wee babby.

The fact that friendships often exist in seasons doesn't diminish the validity of your bond or tarnish any of the memories you've shared with your friends. It's physically impossible to maintain all of your close friendships at once the longer that life goes on.

We're also strong believers that friendships can exist in seasons (plural) rather than a season (singular). Like the seasons of weather, friendships can come in and out of our lives multiple times. These friendships can often cross into the lifetime category. In the latter case, the intensity of your friendship may come and go, but the actual friendship is a constant in your life.

Life lessons from our chicks

Real-life wisdom fresh from our DMs

Some people are only here for a chapter in your story.

Long-distance friendships

Al has had three best friends, *three*, move away. Melbourne, New Zealand and Ireland are all on the naughty list for claiming three of her people.

However, just because a friend is no longer 'just down the road', that doesn't mean that the friendship is over. This is not an easy lesson to learn.

Distance is often completely new terrain to traverse in a friendship. You go from seeing the person every day at work or home or for regular weekend catch-ups to having to book in a Zoom call. It sucks.

First off, if your friend is moving away, allow yourself time to mourn. When Al's lifelong best friend Cassie told her she was moving to Melbourne with her family, Al was so heart-broken she had to leave their slumber party to go home and feel her feelings. To put it dramatically, it felt like she was being abandoned. Then, when her soulmate/roommate Sidnee got her dream job in New Zealand, she spent an entire month before Sidnee moved crying and mourning. When her adopted Irish little sister, Helena, decided to move back home, Al made a PowerPoint presentation of reasons she should stay.

Obviously a long-distance friend is not abandoning you, but when you're in those emotions it can feel a lot like it. Taking a moment to understand how you feel about the situation will allow you to communicate healthily with your friend. Because as hard as it is to reconcile, the friendship is about to change, and there is a type of mourning that comes with that. The inner saboteur voice might come out and start telling you how your best friend is going to find a 'new' best friend and that you're going to grow apart.

Let's debunk that.

Firstly, yes, your friend is going to make new friendships, and that's amazing. You don't want the people you care about to be alone, twiddling their thumbs in complete isolation. Their new friendships do not take away from the one you have. Reminding yourself that your connection is unique and special will allow you to keep hold of your friendship. Secondly, just because they're moving away does not mean your friendship is going to fizzle.

If you are the person who is moving away to live your main character fantasy, understand that this will be hard for your friends who feel 'left behind'.

Once you process your emotions, you ultimately come out the other end and want to support the person you care about. Start celebrating this exciting part of your person's life, as they're going on their next big adventure.

The trickiest part of all long-distance relationships is staying in touch. Al has trudged through this obstacle course with three of her friends and is still close with all of them. Yes, they have seasons where they don't talk for a while, sometimes even a couple of months, but when they do catch up, it's like no time has passed. It's the best feeling in the world: chatting or even seeing your long-distance friend and feeling like nothing has changed. They're still them, you're still you!

So, what's the best way to stay in touch with a long-distance friend? It's not very sexy, but put in a Zoom calendar invite. Even better, make it a recurring time so that you know every first Thursday of the month you grab a bottle of wine and park it on a video call to talk smack with your bestie.

Catching up with your friends shouldn't feel like a chore, work meeting or obligated check-in. Keeping it top line can make the conversation feel like work. We recommend avoiding the simple 'Hey, how are you?' or 'So what's new?' Instead, tell them about the weird takeaway you had that did *not* sit well or how you got oil on your favourite vintage blazer. Better yet, send them memes or funny TikToks between Zoom calls to keep the conversation flowing and let them know you're thinking of them.

Psychologist and friendship expert Marisa G. Franco says that a simple hack to maintaining friendships over a long distance is to develop an anchor—a common interest that acts as a trigger for you to reach out to each other. Whether it's the latest episode of *Love Island* or your love language is sending new song finds to each other, developing this anchor will make contact more casual, easy and freeing.

Anchors helped many of us through the pandemic. In our case, lockdown was the most time we'd ever spent apart. It was *horrible*, to put it mildly. We thought we were going to break out into a rash from the separation anxiety. Dramatic but true. We started doing Zoom parties for every new episode of *RuPaul's Drag Race*. Every Saturday we'd get on Zoom and count 'three, two, one' and start watching at the same time. We felt so connected, even from afar. Having an anchor allows you to develop more intimacy, with inside jokes that are just between the two of you.

Even when you set up times to call ahead of time, life gets busy. Understand that just because you're available at the time doesn't mean your friend always is. Don't overthink it if your friend takes a week to reply to your message. Putting pressure on your friend to be there round the clock is only going to create distance in the relationship and make it feel hard. It's not personal, it's just life.

In a lot of cases, the scales of effort can differ. You may find yourself putting in a lot of effort trying to find time with your long-distance friend but it's not being reciprocated. In this instance, the best thing you can do is be honest and vulnerable with them, even if it feels uncomfortable. A lot of the time, people are in their own head and don't realise how their actions are affecting those around them.

However, in some instances, you may need to accept people can drift apart, and that season of friendship may have run its course. It's not to say that you'll never speak again: some friendships have peaks and valleys and you might come back together at a later time. This can be difficult to accept, but coming to terms with it will only help you grow in the long run.

As you navigate the new normal that is a long-distance friendship, remember to take care of yourself. It is sad. It is hard. Your person is still your person but not in the same way as they used to be and adjusting to that can feel incredibly isolating. Take care of yourself while you adjust, and also take advantage of the opportunity to spend time learning new hobbies and developing new relationships.

All friendships take effort. It's a lie that friendships are 'good vibes only'. Keeping a friendship strong, especially a long-distance one, means reaching out, being honest, finding time and showing how much they're a valued part of your life.

A note from Al

From lifetime, to seasonal, to reason and back to lifetime. That's how my friendship with Cassie has evolved. I'll reveal a little later as to why my friendship with Cass is so important to me, but calling her my best friend has easily been a highlight of my life—even though our friendship has not necessarily been linear.

As mentioned earlier, Cassie and I were best friends, and then she moved to Melbourne. We made the long distance work as much as we could—scheduling phone calls and visiting each other as often as possible on an eighteen-year-old's salary—but our season of being best friends in the same city was over.

As time went by, a few cracks and slips caused us to slowly fizzle. One big one was when I accidentally sent a text to Cassie about how much I hated her then-boyfriend. It was my own karma for not talking to her about it directly, but fuck me was that a blunder. Another was when Cass visited Sydney but had an incredibly busy schedule that didn't account for quality time with me. In complete fairness, I do understand that she had other priorities, but at the time I still felt hurt.

After some time our communication dissolved and it became a reason friendship. There was no anger or animosity between us; I felt a lot of happiness for everything our friendship taught me.

Then, out of the blue, I got a message from Cass saying she was visiting Sydney and wanted to catch up. I can't tell you how happy and nervous I was. It had been years and we were different people—or, at least, I was. I suddenly felt a bit insecure, wondering whether things would be weird between us. We arranged to meet at my place, and I think I bought every type of cheese, cracker, dip, olive and salsa possible out of sheer nerves. When my apartment buzzer rang, my stomach did a flip.

But as soon as I opened the door, it was like I had time travelled. It truly felt like no time had passed since I last saw her. We remembered inside jokes that we hadn't thought of for years. We told stories until we were holding our stomachs, begging the other to stop.

I think a little part of me healed that night on my blue IKEA couch with a giant antipasti board.

We both felt like we were back where we were supposed to be. We apologised for any hurt we caused each other, as unintentional as it was, and both put ourselves out there, saying we wanted to be in each other's lives again.

After that it was never long between visits. Even if it has been a few weeks since our last in-depth chat, it always feels as though no time has passed, and no love is ever lost. She's back in my life for good. Even though our friendship has changed over the years, the fact that we came back together shows how much our friendships can evolve.

Low-maintenance friendships

We've been raised by the likes of *Friends*, *Sex and the City*, *Seinfeld* and *The OC* to think that healthy relationships mean you live in each other's pockets. According to those shows, it's totally normal to rock up to your friend's place unannounced, get coffee after work every day and source romantic relationships from your friendship group. While we know this is a glamorised version of what friendships look like, it still influences the expectations we put on ourselves and our friends in our twenties, thirties and beyond. On top of that, seeing others' friendship commitments advertised constantly on social media can have us questioning the health and validity of our own relationships.

Perhaps this is why the concept of low-maintenance friendships took off on TikTok in 2022. The term refers to friendships that require low touch or less engagement. A low-maintenance friendship is not less valid, it's just different. It allows for the varying levels of engagement people may prefer. While one person may find exchanging podcast-level voice note updates throughout the day a fulfilling way to stay in touch with their friends, others may find that kind of commitment exhausting. We often see collective sighs of relief in the comment sections of TikToks discussing the low-maintenance dynamic. People who had previously felt like bad friends or socially inept feel validated seeing a different type of connection reflected back to them.

Sometimes low-maintenance friendships come from a mutual boundary. For instance, some people need more alone time to recharge their batteries. (Shout out to our li'l introverts out there.) But sometimes low-maintenance friendships are a product of circumstance or necessity, such as when friends move overseas, change jobs or start a family.

There is a fine line between a low-maintenance friendship and one that has run its course, but we think the big difference is whether the relationship still fills your cup. As long as you can still rely on each other when it really counts and you have a mutual understanding of the friendship dynamic, there's no reason why a low-maintenance friendship can't last a lifetime.

However, we want to put a big red underline beneath 'mutual understanding'. We had a conversation with a friend recently who thought she was in a healthy, mutually understood low-maintenance friendship. Turns out, she was not. She hadn't spoken to her friend for about six months, believing they had an agreement that they were in a low-maintenance friendship. Instead, it turns out her friend was super pissed at her for not making any effort and letting the comms drop off.

So if you're in a low-maintenance friendship, it's probably best to check in on your mate to make sure you're both on the same page. This is also why it's so important to understand your friends' love languages and attachment styles, which we'll dig into later in the book.

What to do when a friendship season ends

When a friendship season is drawing to a close, you find yourself at a fork in the road with two options to pursue.

The first option is reigniting the friendship. We believe that some friendships follow their own seasons, and friends can come back into your life naturally or if you pursue them. If you miss a friendship that has fizzled and you feel like you have the capacity to reinvest in it, you should reach out. Try not to get caught up in who sent the last text or who instigated the last catch-up.

If you feel like the friendship was always one-sided, that's okay. You can leave those friendships in the past if you want. But if you *really* care about the friendship, this is something you can resolve within yourself. Sometimes you just need to let go of your pride and be the bigger person. Sadly, we've both witnessed friendships that have ended simply because both sides were too proud to send the 'Hey, how've been?' text. If a text feels like too much, you can test the waters and comment on one of their social media posts. It sounds trivial, we know. But if they reciprocate, it's a sign that they probably miss you too and there's no bad blood.

Speaking of bad blood: if a friendship season comes to an end because of conflict, that's a whole other kettle of fish with its own strategy. Flip to Chapter 5 for some assistance in that department.

If you're trying to enter a new season with a friend, you should also set realistic expectations for yourself. Even if you and your friend reconnect, your friendship probably won't return to exactly how it was. Change is scary, so be kind to yourself and give yourself space to feel some kinda way if the friendship is a little different to before. Just remember that change isn't always a bad thing. Who knows, this could be a positive change for your friendship. Let's say you used to hang out with your old housemate every day and you lost touch after you moved out. A less intense friendship that doesn't rely on hanging out every day will be more sustainable for the long-term. If your friendship now looks like texting weekly and getting a coffee every couple of months, and you're both happy with this arrangement, that's a win in our books.

The second option at the fork in the friendship road is moving on. Sometimes the friendship has run its course and the best thing to do is to let it go. If this is the case, you don't necessarily have to do anything except come to terms with what has happened. It's natural to feel guilt or sadness that it's over, but you could also try to lean into feeling grateful for the amazing memories that you have with that person. If you're feeling isolated or lonely without the friendship, try journalling or reaching out to another friend or professional to air your thoughts. It's also an amazing time to reconnect with yourself. Take yourself on solo dates, invest in your own hobbies and interests and start romanticising your alone time. (In case you need a refresher, we cover exactly how to do this in extensive detail in Chapter 1.)

It's also an exciting opportunity to put yourself out there to make new friends, or put more energy into existing relationships. A friendship season coming to an end is a good reminder not to put all of your friendship eggs in one basket.

So, while it can be sad when a friendship season comes to a close, hopefully you can look back on your time with that person with fondness, and know it could be the catalyst for another incredible chapter in your life.

A lifetime

TL;DR A lifetime friendship is just that: a friendship that goes the distance and lasts a lifetime.

As we've established, most friendships don't survive the test of time. But if you're lucky, you'll make some friends who are stuck with you for life. These friends aren't necessarily people you see or talk to every day, but they are a constant fixture in your life. They're the family you can always go home to.

How many friends can we expect to keep for a lifetime? Because there are so many factors that impact the number and tenure of our friendships, there isn't much concrete evidence on this. But, according to professor of psychology and neuroscience Julianne Holt-Lunstad, somewhere between three to six lifetime friends is the sweet spot. Personally, we'd be happy with even one lifetime friend. When it comes to friendships, we believe in quality over quantity.

At the time of writing this book, we're in our late twenties and early thirties. So it would be naive of us to think that we've learned everything we need to know about lifelong friendships. Let's face it, we still have a lot of life to live and hopefully many more friends to make. However, even a third of the way through life, there are some friendships that we *know* will be with us until the end.

Even though we finish each other's sentences and are basically the same person split into two, we both have very different experiences with lifelong friends.

A note from Sal

I've truly had a best friend since birth: my older sister Meg.

With roughly three-and-a-half years between us, we've always been incredibly close. Perhaps this is because we shared a room for the first thirteen years of my life. Probably to the relief of our older brother, it meant that we were there to entertain (and annoy) each other 24/7 during those formative years. This could have had one of two outcomes: we'd forge an unbreakable bond or end up killing each other. Luckily for us, it was the former.

As well as the identical cackle we inherited from our mum, we have almost all of the same interests, share a lot of mutual friends and are communicating via at least three different apps at most points throughout the day.

Like any good friendship, it's not just our similarities that connect us but our differences as well. Like two sides of the same coin, where she's soft and forgiving, I'm strong-headed and a bit more ruthless. In moments that I'm seeing the glass half empty, she fills it up with her ability to see the silver lining on everything. You get the picture: she's the yin to my yang. It's almost like we're from the same gene pool or something (wink, wink).

And as far as big sisters go, I've lucked out. It's not lost on me that not everyone has such a close friendship with their sibling. We definitely had our squabbles growing up, but for the most part I've always felt an incredible sense of safety with my sister. It's an amazing feeling knowing that there is always going to be at least one person in your corner, no matter what. It's a different type of unconditional love that you don't always get from your other types of friends. It also makes family reunions with distant relatives who say 'I haven't seen you since you were this big!' slightly more bearable.

However, I also believe that even if you do love your family, you don't always have to like them. So even if you weren't born with your very own built-in best friend like I was, take comfort knowing that a lot of people find that unconditional love from friends who aren't related by blood. These friends become your family.

You can meet people who will become lifetime friends at any point in your life. Just because you're not still in touch with that one kid you bonded with in the sandpit on the first day of kindy, it doesn't mean that all hope is lost and you'll never find your friend for life. In fact, you could be blocking yourself off from some life-changing friendships with that attitude. Alex and some of the core friendships she's made in her mid-to-late twenties are proof that finding your forever friends later in life is very much possible.

Like low-maintenance friendships, lifetime friends can go weeks, months or years without seeing each other without it hurting the friendship. Even if you do go for stretches of time without speaking, when you do reconnect it's like no time has passed and the friendship can pick up as normal. That's because your friendship is rooted in a deeper connection that doesn't rely on constant contact to remain alive.

Lifetime friends are the people you consider when you're thinking about your future. For example, if you're considering moving overseas you think about the impact that will have on your friendship. When you picture your wedding day, they're the people posing with you in your photos. If you both talk about kids, you imagine how your children will inevitably end up besties. Regardless of what this looks like for you, the point is that you're likely planning your life with room for these friendships.

If you're friends for life, you've likely had your fair share of tiffs. Lifetime friends don't just fold and take it when it comes to conflict. They know how to handle the inevitable friction of friendship and probably have specific strategies that work for their dynamic. This also means that if your friend says they're sorry, they mean it. If they say you're forgiven, they mean it. That's because lifetime friends are willing to release grudges and grow together, because the future of their friendship means more than winning an argument.

There is one step above lifetime friends in our opinion: your platonic soulmate. This type of friendship doesn't take away from your other lifetime friendships, but it's an even deeper level of connection beyond this. We dig into exactly what your platonic soulmate is in Chapter 10, but we'll give you some examples here to give you an idea of what we mean as a little taste test for now.

While your lifetime friends may be in your wedding party, your platonic soulmate is your person of honour. Your lifetime friends are up-to-date on the latest in your life, but your platonic soulmate is the first friend you call. You can go periods of time without speaking to your lifetime friends, but if you did the same with your platonic soulmate you'd probably break out in a rash.

From reasons, to seasons, to lifetimes: not all friendships are made equal.

Some friendships are lifers, and some are life-changing.

The 'friends forever' vows

Given many friendships are lifelong bonds that outlast other important (even romantic) relationships, we think it's unjust that there isn't a commitment ceremony for friends.

Fun fact: on our first trip to America together, we thought it would be a good idea to elope in Vegas. We were looking into Elvis celebrants and everything, until we realised that it could actually be legally binding and might've been kind of insulting to our boyfriends at the time.

Anyway, to right that wrong, we've created our own friendship vows to bond you and your friend until death do you part:

In the name of Two Broke Chicks, I [your name] *take you* [your friend's name] *to be my friend for life. To side-eye and snort with laughter from this day forward, through hangovers and break-ups, in questionable fashion choices and memories we'll never forget, to love and to cherish, till death do us part. This is my solemn vow.*

Read this out at your next pre-drinks with your pals and by the power vested in us, we pronounce you: friends for life.

A note from Sal

One particular friendship comes to mind when I think of the seasonal and lifetime friendship categories.

Nikita and I have been friends for over 20 years now, which far exceeds the seven-year theory we spoke about earlier in this chapter. We met on my first day at a new primary school, when I made the move mentioned earlier from Sydney's Sutherland Shire to Wollongong.

Nikita had heard there was a new girl showing up, and there was a spare seat next to her in class. So, she came to school with body glitter carefully placed across her cheeks and her hair twisted into space buns. She was ready to impress. And impressed I was.

We became friends instantly. We'd spend our weekends making up dances and stealing clothes from my big sister's closet when she wasn't home. We joined the same netball team and held each other as we cried when we lost the grand final match in Year 4. She's a Cancer and I'm a Pisces, so that checks out. We also bonded over music. We would bring a mixed bag of Britney Spears, Nelly, Elvis and Beach Boys CDs to school and persuade our teacher to let us play them in the classroom at lunchtime.

We even entered a 'best friends' competition hosted by *Total Girl* magazine. We staged our own photo shoot dressed as a devil (her) and angel (me) and submitted it with a paragraph waxing lyrical about why we'd be best friends forever. Part of me wishes I could unearth those photos, but another part of me is glad we took them on a disposable camera and the only copies were sent off to the magazine. To our surprise, we won! Our prize? Season one of *The Simple Life* (the reality TV show starring iconic besties Paris Hilton and Nicole Richie) on DVD. Life was good.

We both went to the same high school and, for the most part, stayed extremely close. However, as best friends who are like sisters do, we fought on and off over the years. Sometimes they were small tiffs and other times they were pretty big blow-ups, which I now really regret and wish I could take back.

But whether we went days or, at one point in Year 12, months without speaking, we'd always come back together. We'd apologise, hug it out and pick up right where we left off. Luckily, we haven't had a fight since our angsty teen days, but that doesn't mean our friendship hasn't continued to evolve over the years.

When we were in our early twenties, we moved into a terrace house full of character in Sydney's inner west. It was the first time I'd moved out of home and the experience was exactly how I imagined living in the city in your twenties would be. We'd spend every Friday night drinking vodka apples at the now-closed Frankie's Pizza on Hunter Street and every hungover Saturday searching for a soul-reviving brekkie and good bargain at Glebe Markets. While I love living with my partner these days, those were some of the most fun years of my life. During that time it was very rare to see me and Nikita apart.

After about eighteen months of living together, Nikita started dating someone and moved in with him within a few months. I wasn't quite ready for our time as housemates to end, but I could hardly blame her for wanting to upgrade from our mould-ridden terrace and take the next step in their relationship at the time.

Once we moved out, though, our friendship entered another new era. We went from seeing each other every day, to every other week and then month. As often happens when you're not chatting face to face regularly, the comms slowly dropped off. Although our friendship had taken on many forms in the past, going from practically inseparable to barely seeing each other shook me a little (though I had also become shit on the replies).

After a couple of my texts to her went unanswered, I started to worry about the status of our friendship. After a lot of mulling, I eventually reached out, saying I hadn't heard from her in a while and wanted to see if she was okay and whether I'd unknowingly done something to upset her. It turned out the unanswered texts had nothing to do with me. She was just up to her eyeballs in work, and life was a little chaotic at the time.

We caught up for coffee not long after and it was like no time had passed. After hearing her side of the conversation, I also realised and acknowledged that I hadn't been a perfect friend either. I had been preoccupied with work and other relationships with my life. As such, I'd probably been taking our friendship for granted and hadn't been devoting the level of attention that it deserved.

This conversation taught me to have more empathy and patience with other friendships and recognise when I, myself, need to put in more effort. Most of the time, this stuff isn't personal. Life can get busy, and just because your friendship looks a little different now, it doesn't take away from any memories you've had or are yet to make. Just like individuals, friendships are supposed to change and grow as life goes on, and while it can be unsettling it's also totally natural.

Since that coffee with Nikita all of those years ago, we've both made an effort to stay in touch and spend time together more regularly. Sometimes we find ourselves stuck in busy periods when a text every other week is still enough to maintain our friendship. And, like usual, whenever we reunite, we can pick up where we left off.

That's because this friendship is for a lifetime. Our friendship isn't seasonal in the sense that it isn't ongoing, but it *has* had seasons within it. From playing with Bratz dolls in my childhood bedroom to causing mischief as teenagers and moving in together, and now battling the throes of our thirties side by side, our friendship has changed yet remained a constant throughout it all.

Dear Sal and Al

Should I reach out to my best friend of six years even if we haven't spoken in months? Or is it time to let it go?

We've both been here, chick, and it sucks. So firstly, we're sending big cuddles your way.

It's difficult to give specific advice without knowing exactly what has happened. Perhaps something caused a rift between you two, or maybe life has just gotten busy and you've found yourselves naturally drifting?

Without knowing all of the juicy details, we'd say it's time to reach out to your friend. Unless your friendship turned particularly sour or toxic, there's no reason why you can't mend the bond. The fact that you're writing in and asking for advice shows that you miss your friend and you don't yet have closure in the relationship. If it's just that you two have drifted over the last few months, it's not worth letting six years of friendship go, in our opinion.

It's totally normal for friendships to ebb and flow as time goes on. So perhaps your friendship with this person isn't over, but it has entered a new era and you're both experiencing some teething issues with this shift.

All friendship dynamics are very different. As we get older and life grows busier, it's a pretty common experience for some best friends not to speak for weeks or months at a time. Then, when they reconnect, it's like no time has passed and they can pick up as normal.

If you've suddenly gone from being best friends glued at the hip to not speaking for months, we can understand feeling a bit nervous or awkward about that. But if you want your bestie back, you've just gotta rip the bandaid off. Send them a text or call them and address the elephant in the room. If you're not sure where to start, here's a loose script to work with:

Hey bestie, I'm sorry it has been so long since we spoke. I really miss you and would love to catch up. Want to meet for a [coffee/cocktail/phone call/coastal walk] *this weekend?*

It can honestly be that simple! Don't over-complicate it or keep putting it off. When you catch up, you can explain why you didn't reach out earlier and hopefully that'll encourage them to do the same so you can both move on. After that, try to schedule regular catch-ups—whether it's fortnightly phone calls or weekly coffees—to get the friendship back on track to where you both want it to be.

If you reach out and your friend doesn't respond, it could be a sign to leave the ball in their court. That way you at least know you tried and you can hopefully get some closure to move on.

Sending you lots of good vibes and the best of luck, lovely!

Lots of love,

Sal and Al

FRIENDSHIP LOVE LANGUAGES

GIFT
TOUCH
WORDS
SERVICES
TIME

We're sure you've heard of love languages: the five different ways people show and experience love. While the discussion of love languages has certainly made the rounds in recent years, it's not a new concept.

The term was originally coined by author Gary Chapman in his 1992 book *The Five Love Languages: How to Express Heartfelt Commitment to Your Mate*. According to Chapman, the five love languages include:

- words of affirmation
- quality time
- gifts
- acts of service
- physical touch.

This theory is far from perfect. It's not backed by science and is written through a heteronormative lens. People can't (and shouldn't) be placed in strict boxes; human emotions are certainly more nuanced than a list you can tick off with one hand. In fact, you may find that you express and receive love through a combination of the love languages or in ways that expand beyond the five listed in Chapman's book. However, we do think it's helpful to acknowledge the ways in which you and the people around you like to give and receive love.

This is because we've personally found that you can experience a more reciprocally fulfilling relationship by understanding someone else's prime love language(s). That way you have a better understanding of what to do or say to make your other half feel loved.

The love languages are typically used to describe how people exchange affection in (largely hetero and cis) romantic relationships exclusively. However, we believe that love languages apply to platonic relationships as well. That's because, just like in a romantic relationship, there are things that we need to express and receive from a friendship to feel fully seen, supported and loved.

In terms of our own friendship, we're both big physical touch girlies. Whenever one of us is upset, the other knows that they need to be squeezed in a cuddle of anaconda-level proportions immediately. However, if your best friend is more of a words of affirmation type, a pep talk might do them more good than a casual spoon.

We've all seen the dynamic of two besties who seem like polar opposites. Maybe one friend is a total cuddle bunny and must be physically glued to their mate at all times, while the other friend would rather eat their own purse than show such raucous displays of affection. While an ideal friendship doesn't have to consist of people with identical love languages, it's important to at least be aware so you can make a conscious effort to do things that'll give your friends the warm and fuzzies.

To help you show your friends love based on their love language, we're going to break down the five love languages, what they mean and how they apply to friendships.

Words of affirmation

The first love language is words of affirmation. This translates to verbal or written expressions of love, compliments and praise— basically saying how the fuck you feel with your words. If this is your friend's love language, they'll feel supported by regular communication, validated by verbal praise and inspired by words of encouragement.

Friends who appreciate this love language will pen birthday cards that'll make you cry. They're the ones who won't leave an interaction without saying 'Love you!' followed by a swift demand of 'Say it back!' They're quick to compliment your outfit even when you're wearing an old One Direction T-shirt and coffee-stained trackies (not because they're lying, but because they genuinely think you're always looking cute).

If you're not super comfortable sharing how you feel in words, there are heaps of ways to show your friend love that don't require you to recite a monologue every time you see them (although, that's not a bad idea if you're down).

How to show your friends love: words of affirmation edition

Write them a letter

Whether it's a Post-it note telling them you're proud of them or a heartfelt letter listing your favourite memories together, this is the way to your friend's heart. If the thought of writing regular letters is making your hand cramp up, you can always save this for special occasions such as their birthday or when they're going through a particularly hard time. Bonus points if it's written on some cute stationery.

Check up on them regularly

For this pal, sending a funny TikTok accompanied by a message that says 'This is so us' once a week probably isn't going to cut it every time. Instead, check in on them regularly and make time to catch up. Your friend shows and feels love through meaningful conversation, not rushed chitchat before heading into a movie. Pick a time and place that's quiet. If it's a long-distance friendship, lock in a regular time to call or FaceTime when you won't be distracted and can get into a juicy chat.

Shower them in compliments

When you think of a compliment in your head, say it out loud. There are the obvious ones such as 'I love how you're wearing your hair today' or 'Your outfit is amazing', but compliments don't always have to be about physical appearance.

Here are some ideas to get you started:

- ☺ You have the best laugh.
- ☺ I always have the most fun nights out with you.
- ☺ You're an amazing cook.
- ☺ I always feel so happy after we hang out.
- ☺ You always make people feel so welcome.
- ☺ I love how you're never afraid to speak up for yourself.
- ☺ You have the best taste in movies.
- ☺ I'm so proud of you!
- ☺ You always inspire me.
- ☺ I really appreciate you.

Be honest with them

The phrase 'honesty is the best policy' is especially true in this case. That's because open communication is the foundation of friendship for this type of pal. Even in a difficult conversation, being honest and clear will help them feel respected.

Practise gratitude

To be honest, we should be doing this with all of our friends regardless of their love language. However, verbally expressing your thanks goes a long way with a friend who appreciates words of affirmation. Tell them the things you appreciate about them as a friend and thank them when they go out of their way to do something for you.

Quality time

If your friend's love language is quality time, they prioritise spending time with the people they love. This means giving and receiving undivided attention and making time for meaningful interactions that'll strengthen your bond. Going to brunch and spending the whole time on your phone doesn't count.

This is the friend who makes plans to ensure the girls' weekend away actually makes it out of the group chat. It's the friend who would prefer tickets to an experience together over an expensive piece of jewellery on their birthday. It's also the friend with whom you can sit comfortably in silence without feeling awkward.

How to show your friends love: quality time edition

Be present

When you're spending time with this friend, try to limit distractions as much as possible. Pick a quiet location where you can have long, interrupted conversations. Put your phone on do not disturb and in your bag (or, even better, in a separate room). This type of friend also appreciates one-on-one time together, so make sure you book in solo catch-ups as well as group hangs.

Use active listening skills

This friend will feel most appreciated when you provide them with undivided attention. If you're the type of person who finds your mind wandering mid-conversation or tends to focus on what you're going to say next instead of actually listening (mood), read on.

Six tips for active listening

1. Face your friend and make eye contact

If you can, sit across from your friend or turn your body towards them to signal that you're paying attention and invested in the conversation. As they're talking, avoid looking at your phone or around you, and maintain comfortable eye contact. Ideally, you should be maintaining eye contact for 50 per cent of the time when you're speaking and 70 per cent when you're listening. If you don't feel super comfortable maintaining eye contact, you can also look at their mouth, nose or chin so your body language matches your investment in the conversation.

2. Pay attention to non-verbal cues

Words are just one part of a conversation. Often your friend's tone of voice, facial expressions and body language can tell you a lot about how they are really feeling.

3. Don't interrupt

Sometimes interrupting comes from a place of excitement, but avoid jumping into the conversation before your friend has finished speaking. Instead, make note of what you wanted to add and bring it up once they've finished.

4. Listen without judgement

Remember that, like yourself, your friend is a human with perspectives, experiences and flaws. And that's why you love them! You can share your own opinions, but try to listen without judgement, jumping to conclusions or imposing your own thoughts. Give your friend the space to share how they're feeling.

5. Don't start planning what to say next

The goal of active listening is to listen to understand, not to respond. You can't properly absorb what your friend is saying if you're rehearsing what you'll say next in your head. Make an effort to take in what they're saying and form your response once they've said their piece. It's not a race and you can take your time!

6. Show you're listening

As well as maintaining eye contact and putting your phone down, nodding along as they speak and asking questions can help your friend feel seen and heard.

Schedule regular catch-ups

Organising time to hang out with friends can feel harder than playing Jenga after a few cocktails. If your friend's love language is quality time, it's important to weather the back-and-forth of 'I can't do Friday. What about Sunday next week? Oh, you're busy Sunday next week. What about Wednesday four years from now?' If you struggle with the back-and-forth, do yourself a favour and book in a regular time to catch up with your friend.

For example, Al loves to host Taco Tuesday for a bunch of her friends every week. She also has a regular FaceTime booked in with her best friend, who lives in New Zealand, every Sunday afternoon.

Create core memories together

Quality time lovers yearn to make lifelong memories with their friends. Grabbing coffee or bingeing your favourite show together is nice, but you should also make an effort to travel together, see live music, explore new places in your hometown and whatever other core-memory–making moments tickle your fancy.

Gifts

This one is pretty self explanatory: if your friend's love language is gifts, they feel and receive love by way of presents. The gifts don't have to be expensive or grand gestures. Instead, they should be thoughtful and sentimental.

This is the friend who always gives *the* best birthday presents. They're the person you secretly hope gets you in Secret Santa. They're the one who will grab you your favourite coffee without you having to ask before they come over. They're the one who will return to the car from the petrol station with your favourite choccie in hand. The presents they love to give and receive are always from the heart and, to them, they are a sign that you're thinking of one another.

How to show your friends love: gifts edition

Make them a playlist

Nothing quite says 'I love you' like making a custom playlist. Making playlists is a love language in itself for Sal. Here are some playlist themes you could create for a friend:

- Songs that remind me of you.
- The soundtrack to the movie about your life.
- Your celebrity crushes in a playlist.
- We're going on a road trip and grabbing Maccas for breakfast.
- Songs that could've been written about you.

Create a photo album of memories

A scrapbook or photo book of memories is the type of sentimental present that'll play the slap bass on your friend's heart strings. It's a gift they can keep for life and continue adding to, and it's a tangible way to show how much you appreciate your memories together.

Al once surprised Sal with a scrapbook from our first trip to America together, including (often questionable) photos, Broadway ticket stubs and other mementos from the trip. It resulted in many tears and giggles, and is something that Sal digs out to flip through whenever she needs a quick hit of dopamine.

Surprise them with gifts

You don't have to wait till their birthday to treat this friend. Waiting for birthdays and Christmas is like torture for them.

There's no better feeling than giving someone a small gift and saying, 'This reminded me of you.' It doesn't need to be big. Grab your work wife a coffee on your way to the office. Shout your friend dinner for no reason. Pick up a cute bunch of flowers before you catch up at your mate's place. Spontaneous gifts don't need to be expensive or extravagant, but they will show your friend you were thinking about them and they'll bloody love you for it.

Acts of service

The acts of service love language is based on doing things to make life easier, more enjoyable or less stressful for your friend. This shows that you pay attention to their needs, actively think about them and make conscious efforts to help them out.

This is the friend who offers to help you pack when you're moving apartments. It's the one who invites you over and makes you your favourite meal when they know you've had a hectic week at work. It's the friend who will pick up some groceries and medicine when you're feeling under the weather.

How to show your friends love: acts of service edition

You can get creative here based on your friend's wants and needs. To get you started, here are ten ways you can conduct acts of service that'll make your friend feel loved:

1. Help them move house.
2. House-sit.
3. Cook them their favourite meal.

④ Look after their pets when they're away.

⑤ Proofread their texts before a first date.

⑥ Help them do their hair or make-up for a night out.

⑦ Let them borrow your clothes.

⑧ Help plan and book logistics when travelling.

⑨ Run errands together.

⑩ Drive them to the airport.

Physical touch

If your friend's love language is physical touch, they're big into giving and receiving physical closeness and affection.

This is the friend who gives *the* best bear hugs. The one who loves skipping down the street hand in hand. The one who insists on sleepovers with plenty of spooning (or is that last one just us?). They love showering their friends with smooches and don't save physical affection just for their romantic partners. (Of course, always ask for consent and show physical affection within their comfortable boundaries.)

A note from Sal

One time Al and I were on a dolphin tour in Hawaii and made friends with one of the tour guides. He admitted he initially didn't approach us because we were cuddling so much that he thought we were dating. He didn't want to interrupt our romantic moment as we admired the island views from the back of the boat. I'd like to say this is the only time we've been mistaken for a romantic couple, but it's not.

How to show your friends love: physical touch edition

Give them lots of cuddles

There's a theory on the internet that true best friends don't *ever* hug. We don't subscribe to this theory, and neither do our fellow fans of physical touch. Hugging when you say hello or goodbye is the absolute minimum with friends who value physical touch. The more spontaneous cuddles you can comfortably offer, the better.

Pro tip: your brain releases maximum levels of oxytocin and serotonin after hugging for more than six seconds. So you should aim for cuddles of six seconds or more if you really wanna get those happy brain chemicals pumping.

Give massages or head scratches

If your friend is feeling stressed or down, a little shoulder and neck massage, arm tickle or head scratch will work wonders to show them you're attentive and there for them. Bonus points if you do this for them when they're hungover. Sal once gave Al a head scratch during the hangover from hell and she never felt more loved.

Hold hands

There's something so heartwarming about skipping down the street hand in hand with your bestie as a grown-arse adult. It's something that we would always do as little kids, but often feel awkward to do as adults. Screw that, we say. Show your physical touch friend some good ol' fashioned PDA!

Sit next to them

You don't even need to be touching necessarily, but sitting next to them at a group setting such as a restaurant or party will help them feel supported by you.

How to identify your friends' love languages

If, after reading these descriptions, you're still feeling a bit clueless about your friends' love languages, there are a few ways to figure it out.

Sometimes it's as simple as watching and learning. You may be able to pinpoint your friends' preferred love languages by observing how they treat their loved ones. This is because people's natural way of showing affection usually mirrors how they like to receive it. For example, if you notice one of your friends is always the first to offer to drive someone to the airport, it's likely that their love language is acts of service.

Some love languages are easier to spot than others. There's also the possibility that your friend may have more than one love language, with one likely sitting at the top of the pecking order. If your friend mirrors traits of a few different love languages, you can always ask them which one is their favourite.

If you want to nail down your bestie's love language to a fine point, you can do a love language quiz online together. The quizzes usually only take a few minutes and ask a series of questions about how and when you feel the most connected to, supported by and close to your loved ones. The results usually include a breakdown of which love language you prefer by percentage, so you'll know exactly how you can honour each other's needs. (This also gives us throwbacks to the quizzes in the back of *Dolly* magazine that we'd do with our besties, and we're here for it.)

Sal and Al's nine friendship love languages (and maybe yours too!)

While the traditional five love languages can be applied to friendship, as we've discussed, we've identified some other love languages that are especially unique to friends. Here are our top nine.

Unwavering justification

We've said it on the podcast and we'll say it here: best friends are basically trained in PR. If this is your friend's love language, there is no spin doctor quite like this ride-or-die. Don't get it twisted, though. They're not afraid to call you out on your shit when you need it. But for the most part, they're the one person who will *always* justify your bad decisions and toxic traits for you. Allow us to illustrate:

You only *just* scraped by on an assignment?
'Ps get degrees anyway.'

Accidentally flirted your way into a situationship . . . again?
'Don't worry, it's character-building for the other person.'

Collecting parking tickets like Pokémon cards?

'It's good for the economy!'

Drunk-texted your ex at 3 am and fell asleep before they even had a chance to reply?

'You can't blame yourself. Mercury is in retrograde again!'

Sharing clothes

If your friend's love language is sharing clothes, they're the type of person who will offer to lend you their new top before they've even worn it. They're basically the group's personal stylist and are always happy to top off any outfit with the perfect accessory from their closet. This person doesn't guilt you when you ask to borrow something and they don't immediately jump in with 'Yeah, it's mine!' when someone compliments their friend for wearing something from their wardrobe. Their motto is 'sharing is caring', and they just want to see their friends looking and feeling their hottest.

Hatred of your toxic ex

Hell hath no fury like a girl whose best friend has just been fucked over by a love interest. If this is your friend's love language, they probably hate your past flings more than you do. Their brain is an organised rolodex of every person who has wronged you, their crimes and fitting punishment should they ever cross paths. Remember when Charlotte York screamed 'I curse the day you were born!' at Mr Big in the first *Sex and the City* movie? That's the energy this friend is bringing.

Truth be told, this friend can be a little scary at times and is probably the last person you want to tell when you're considering giving your ex a second chance. But that's because their love language is based on fierce loyalty for you. They're also going to be the first person to stand up for you, pick you up when you're down and remind you why you're *that* bitch when you're crying over your worm of an ex.

Big sibling dynamic

This is the friend who's the big sister or mother hen of the group. They likely thrive doing acts of service. They're most likely the one who will rally the group chat and organise the most budget-friendly accommodation for the girls' trip. They're the friend who will remind you to drink your eight glasses of water a day. They're also the first one you call when you need sound advice to get out of a sticky situation. This is also the friend who absolutely insists that you text them that you've got home safe after a night out. They're nurturing, thoughtful and reliable.

Sending memes

This is a key love language for any fruitful friendship in the current day. This love language can exist within every type of friendship, from best friends who are glued at the hip to former work wives who go months or years between catch-ups. Underneath the meme that relates to an obscure inside joke, chaotic memory or your most underneath toxic trait is a deeper meaning: 'This made me think of you.' We're being 100 per cent earnest when we say it's one of the purest love languages between friends you can have.

Scrolling on your phone in silence together

It may not sound like much, but this love language is *elite* and reserved for very special friendships. That's because it only applies to friendships so strong that long silences never feel awkward. You can genuinely sit comfortably in silence for long periods without having to fill the air with mundane chatter. Scrolling on your phone is just one example, but this love language can also be extended to reading books together or laying side by side at the beach on a sunny day. These are usually the types of friends who don't drain your social battery, and you can be 100 per cent yourself around them. We're not saying these types of friends will leave you constantly in silence. Instead, they know when to let a conversation breathe, and being with them feels just as comfortable as spending time alone.

Drafting texts

Everyone needs at least one of these friends in their corner. That's because it's common knowledge that texts exchanged in the early stages of dating are basically ghostwritten by a friend. If this is your friend's love language, their brain is full of witty comebacks, and they always employ the perfect use of full stops and exclamation marks. They're also well versed in the fine art of which and how many emojis to use. They study the replies with greater depth and a richer content analysis than your English teacher during the HSC. This is the same friend who probably wants to peer review any updates you plan to make to your dating profile or Instagram captions before they go live.

10/10 recommendations

Catch up with a friend with this love language and they'll give you a long list of books, TV shows, movies and podcasts you simply *have* to watch or listen to. They'll selflessly lend you the box set of their favourite book series and text you regularly asking for an in-depth review of each chapter you read. When you're watching a favourite movie with them, they spend more time watching your face to see your reactions in real time than they do watching the screen. Somehow they know more about your music tastes than you do and have a knack for curating playlists full of songs you've never heard but immediately love.

Having your back

A friend with this love language is otherwise known as a ride-or-die bitch. Not everyone can fill these big and fabulous shoes, but everyone should aim to have one friend with this love language in their inner circle.

This friend is your number-one fucking fan. They'll shout out your life wins and milestone moments on their own Instagram Stories. They'll leave a glowing review of your small business (or, in our case, podcast) for the world to see. They'll sing your praises at a networking opportunity when you'd be the perfect candidate for a new job. They've probably even cosplayed as your past landlord or employer to give you a glowing review when a reference was needed.

They're also super reliable. You know they're going to be the first to click 'attending' on your birthday party invite. You can count on them to pick up the phone at 3 am. Not only will they not participate if they hear people talking smack about you, they'll stand up for you as if it were a personal insult to themselves. They could be offered a billion dollars to spill it all and they'd take your deepest, darkest secrets to the grave. And because they're your ride-or-die bitch, you'd do the bloody same for them.

A note from Sal

Between Al, my big sister and some of my lifelong friends, I feel pretty lucky to have a couple of friends who I would put in this ride-or-die category. One of them is Caroline.

We first became friends when we were assigned neighbouring seats on our first day of Year 7. (It's probably the one and only time alphabetical seating hasn't done someone dirty.) I asked her, 'Do you like Britney Spears?' She promptly replied, 'I love her!' The friendship was instantly a done deal for me. More than eighteen years later she's still one of my best friends.

There are quite a few memories that pop into my mind that make Caroline fit for the ride-or-die category. Like the months she had the patience of a saint when she taught me how to drive so I could get my driver's licence. She survived many parallel-parking–related breakdowns, dropped me off for my test and was waiting for me afterwards with a big grin of encouragement. Both times. (Yes, I failed my first driver's test. Get over it.)

Or the time she held my hair back while I vomited into her parents' sink full of clean dishes after a big night out as a late teen. Not my proudest moment. I'm pretty sure she cleaned up after me, once she'd tucked me safely into her bed of course.

However, the memory that really sticks out to me is the morning after my parents announced they were getting a divorce. Yep. Strap in. I'll save you from the gory details, but it wasn't the most pleasant experience and had been building for a while. As my biggest confidante, Caroline was well and truly informed of my family's dysfunctional dynamic. She probably wasn't super surprised when I texted her the news when it all blew up that night.

Naively but probably relatably, I was heartbroken but also really embarrassed that my parents were breaking up. I can't explain why, because I had known for a long time that they shouldn't be together. Regardless, I asked Caroline not to breathe a word about it to anyone. Without hesitation, she agreed. After a night of no sleep, I rocked up to school with bloodshot eyes. I was determined to keep my brave face and not betray any hint of what was going on. As a teenager, I was super proud (see: stubborn) and didn't like to let people see me in moments of weakness.

As you probably predicted, that plan turned to shit pretty quickly. I arrived at school earlier than Caroline and waited at our usual spot, with my head down and my iPod headphones jammed into my ears. But as I looked up and saw her concerned face walking towards me, I burst into tears. As dozens or maybe even hundreds of fellow students streamed into the school, she shielded me in her arms as I sobbed into her chest. She did her best to both comfort and conceal me, including from a bunch of our friends and classmates who witnessed the outburst.

Despite the unintended commotion I'd caused before homeroom that day, Caroline remained like a steel trap and revealed nothing to anyone. Even when some of our closest friends pulled her aside and asked her what was up, she refused to gossip or give them any information. Although we probably weren't sophisticated enough to articulate it in this way as seventeen-year-olds, she knew I was heartbroken and this was private. She'd made a promise and she intended to keep it. Now that's a ride-or-die bitch.

This level of unwavering loyalty has remained a foundation of our almost-two-decade-long friendship. But, as demonstrated by my friendship with Al, it is possible to find friendships like this well into adulthood as well. So if someone doesn't immediately pop into your head when you think of a ride-or-die friend, don't give up. You just haven't found them yet.

Twenty ways to tell your friends you love 'em without saying 'I love you'

While we personally think it's important to tell your friends 'I love you' every time you see them, you can get more creative than using these three words and eight letters. Or maybe you have the kind of friendship where making a grand declaration of love every time you hang out may feel a bit weird. We don't judge. Regardless of how you feel about it, there are a bunch of ways to demonstrate your appreciation and love for a friend without saying ily.

(1) Ask them to text you when they get home after a night out.
(2) Help them pick out an outfit.

③ Watch their favourite movie with them.

④ Ask them if they've had any interesting dreams lately.

⑤ Shit talk their ex/boss/annoying neighbour with them.

⑥ Offer to do a chore or run an errand they hate for them.

⑦ Bring them their favourite greasy meal when they're hungover.

⑧ Send flowers to them when they're sad, celebrating or just because.

⑨ Compliment them.

⑩ Share their work wins, milestone moments or really hot selfies on social media.

⑪ Buy them a book you think they'd like.

⑫ Be genuinely excited when they share good news.

⑬ Show up to events that are important to them.

⑭ Encourage them to have 'me time' if they're run-down.

⑮ Send them TikToks that will make them laugh.

⑯ Write them a heartfelt letter.

⑰ Ask them for advice.

⑱ Start a new hobby with them.

⑲ Organise a holiday, weekend away or road trip with them.

⑳ Ask them how they're *really* doing.

• •

Everyone gives and wants to receive love in their own ways. The only thing that we all have in common is that we all want to love and be loved. If you reflect on your friendships, we bet you could add heaps of friendship love languages of your own to the list we've shared. That's the beauty of it: there's no one right way to show your friend that you care about them.

It's also important to remember that not everyone gives love the way they want to receive it. Just because they shower you with thoughtful gifts to tell you they love you, doesn't mean that's how they want or expect some platonic lovin' in return.

So pay attention, ask questions and tell your mate that you love them.

MAKING FRIENDS IN ADULTHOOD

'How do I make friends as an adult?' is one of the most common questions we're asked on our podcast, and for good reason: it's fucking hard.

Wanna hang out? Maybe for, like, ever?

Feeling like you lack friendships as an adult is not a comfortable experience. It can feel embarrassing to admit this to ourselves, let alone to other people. Just like in dating, your social circle and status can seem like a reflection of your goodness. To quote icon (and our adoptive mother) Kris Jenner: 'Show me your friends and I'll show you who you are.'

If you don't have a big friendship group, you might wonder whether the common denominator is you. Of course, in most cases it isn't, but it can be hard to move past the self-blame. In some cases, it may be worth looking inwards: you might have some self-love and reflection work to do. But it's also important to remember that finding your people can be genuinely rough—even in this time of instant connection via DMs, Instagram Stories and Messenger group chats.

While social media can be an incredible tool for building connections it can also be a damning one. At this point, we all understand social media is a highlights reel of social interactions. Seriously, it's literally called *social* media. This still doesn't stop us from comparing ourselves to everyone else on it.

Maybe you see some Instagram Stories of a group of friends at a bottomless brunch or multiple posts from a house party and can't help but feel a little bit left out. This is not an uncommon feeling—it's actually an incredibly human feeling.

Research shows that we struggle to make friends at an older age due to a *lack of trust.* Once we're in our twenties and older we feel reluctant to put our trust, feelings and hearts in the hands of someone new. By the time we're adults it's fairly common to have experienced a breach of trust with a friend. We can all remember a time when we've told someone private information only for them to share it with others, or experienced a break-up with a friend or romantic partner that left us feeling a little bit disheartened. We become personal acquaintances of rejection and betrayal, and feel the disappointment of wasting our time on someone. This means the idea of putting ourselves out there for someone else feels overwhelming, and the fear is often what holds us back from finding the people you're meant to.

The experiences we have when we're younger, both negative and positive, form who we are in our twenties and beyond. Al, who struggled to make friends in high school, deeply appreciates her true friends now and has absolutely no time for cliquey dynamics that aren't inclusive. Our early experiences may also cause us to tightly hold on to old friendships that may not be the best thing for our growth anymore. We don't want to throw away the time investment it took to build trust only to 'start again'.

It's a false notion that we need to lose old friendships to make new ones. Making new friends does not lessen or devalue our current ones. No mushroom cloud of a friendship blow-up needs to happen for you to want to expand your connections. No big break-up, drunk altercation, fucked-your-ex or bitched-about-you-on-FaceTime event needs to occur for you to feel like you want to meet new people.

But sometimes the mushroom cloud happens. That's okay, too.

The meandering path you take to find your people is what it is. It has led you to exactly where you're meant to be, because what is meant for you will never miss you.

Stop thinking you have to start again in cultivating friendships and rebrand it to your personal evolution. Think of the first time you watched your favourite TV show or read your favourite novel, and how much you would kill to be able to experience that for the first time again. That's how you're going to feel about finding your people.

Take comfort that these moments you're experiencing right now are the good ol' days that you'll look back on in years to come and wish you were more present. Remember that you're bigger and the world is bigger than whatever anxiety you're feeling right now. Making friends as an adult can be daunting, but it can also open a whole new world.

Holding on to high school friends

The first day of high school is something many of us remember, whether it was a positive or negative experience. When you think of this time, your mind may be filled with happy memories of friendships that just 'clicked'. Or maybe meeting a bunch of strangers made you feel nervous right down to the pit of your stomach. Perhaps it felt like you were thrown into the animal kingdom and you were on the bottom of the food chain.

Memories of high school friendships are often mixed with an array of emotions. If you found it overwhelming, that's not surprising. When you start at school you're essentially thrown in to socialising with a group of strangers turned potential friends your own age five days a week. The forced proximity sometimes means you make friends with whomever you're assigned to work with on a group assignment. We'd argue that proximity can result in some powerful enemies too. The friends we make at school are those with whom we share the wild and tumultuous journey of adolescence—periods, hormones, first kisses, break-ups, parties and part-time jobs.

People always say that the teen years with high school friends are the 'golden days'. But what happens if they're not?

A note from Al

I absolutely, positively, wholeheartedly hated high school. I do not look back with nostalgia. In fact, when an invitation to my ten-year reunion hit my inbox, I marked it as spam.

Like a lot of us, I struggled to find where I fit during high school. Fretting about who I'd sit next to on the bus or which cabin I'd be in at school camp would literally keep me up at night for hours.

During the first four years of high school I was trying to be friends with people I really thought I wanted to be friends with. You know, the girls who made an acronym with all their names and called their group that? I tried my hardest to be liked by these popular girls for reasons that are completely lost to me now. But when we're thrust into the zoo that is the lunchtime schoolyard, all logical thinking goes out the window.

What I'm saying is, making friends can be hard. Especially in high school.

When I was sixteen, the cracks started to show. I so badly wanted to be accepted by these people yet I didn't know if I even liked them.

Shit hit the fan when the relentless bullying started. One lunchtime, everyone ran away from me whenever I tried to sit down. I found out later it was because the girls had spread a rumour I had nits. (Seriously. We were 16.)

After a school camp, I received a text telling me to throw away my toiletries because the girls had stolen them and dunked them all in a toilet. Facebook statuses described things they'd do to me at lunchtime the next day—none of them good.

The twelve months after I'd 'left the group' was one of the hardest periods of my life. I could barely muster the energy to go to school. I was genuinely scared of these girls. They would incite reactions from me that were sad and angry, and regretfully there were times I'd sink to their level and say nasty things in an attempt to try to stand up for myself or pretend like it didn't affect me like it did.

But it wasn't all bad. This experience led me to find three friends, one of whom was Cassie—the bestie I spoke about in Chapter 2.

These girls saved me in high school. They picked me up and gave me a safe space away from the mess. With them I always had a spot on the bus and somewhere to sit at lunch. With them I was accepted, included and appreciated.

With Cassie I had my first experience of a best friend. This taught me a lot about what it's like to genuinely fall in love with a friend, and what qualities I should seek when I'm making new friends.

As it does, life happened and we all drifted apart a bit after high school—but the lessons I learned from this high school experience have never left me. As much as I never want to experience being bullied again, it taught me that quality is oh so much better than quantity; that friendship is about acceptance, not popularity.

For a while, I thought that my not belonging to a big group of friends in high school might be seen as a red flag in adulthood. That when people asked if I was still close friends with anyone from high school and my response was 'No', I'd be labelling myself as a problem person or stamping 'loser' on my forehead.

Again, this isn't true. It's that naughty little bit of insecurity in my head taking me back to a lunchtime circle where there wasn't space for me to sit.

Just because I didn't belong to a big group in high school and didn't carry dozens of friends into my adult years doesn't mean I'm destined to live a life without friends, that I'm the problem or that I'm just plain unlikeable.

The entire notion that you need to have a friendship group to be acceptable is completely wrong.

Because of my past, I now appreciate my friendships so much more. It was as an adult that I truly found myself and, as a result, found my people.

Do adults need a best friend or core group?

Some fortunate folks are lucky to find lifelong friendships in the earlier years of their lives. This isn't the case for everyone, though, and it's more common than you may think to be starting from scratch in adulthood. High school friendships can dwindle. Moving into adulthood presents hurdles that some friendships cannot make it over—simple life steps such as a gap year, university or getting a full-time job can cause friends to drift in different directions.

When you don't have a core group of friends it's easy to feel like you don't belong. Especially when you're scrolling on Instagram, watching others host fun dinner parties or take on the world with mates on a Euro trip. We found some of our people in our late twenties and, even then, it was a happy accident where a bunch of misfits found each other.

Our current group of friends can only be described as a cluster of weirdos who all genuinely enjoy each other. We all go on little trips away, send memes to the group chat and plan Christmas celebrations together. Who knows if we would even have got along if we'd met each other in high school. We're all grateful we found each other when we did, because we've already learned so much about ourselves and how to be healthy in relationships, so we can actually be good people for one another.

In saying that, you don't need a huge circle of friends. In fact, it's not even plausible to maintain the huge number of friendships that social media suggests we should have.

Quality over quantity

When it comes to friendship, quality trumps quantity. This is a scientific fact.

In the nineties, psychologist Robin Dunbar published a study stating that humans can cognitively handle 150 stable social relationships (including romantic relationships, family and friends). Sorry to old mate Dunbar, but that number truly makes us want to throw up. We don't even have that many friends on Facebook, let alone real life. However, we will throw Dunbar a bone here as he continues on to say that out of dozens of connections, the ideal number of true friendships is five.

A 2020 study of 422 women found the ideal number of close friendships that is actually possible to maintain is three to five. This makes sense to us, especially given that one of the most common barriers to making friends as an adult is lack of time. Between juggling our career, going on dates, spending time with a romantic partner and our family, working out, doing our life admin and spending time on our own, fitting in friends can seem like the hardest and sometimes last thing we want to do. As we get older, we've found that trying to arrange dates with friends old and new feels a little like booking in a dentist appointment.

'Hey, it has been months since I've seen you!'

'Right! Are you free this Saturday?'

'I'm working. But I can do 19 April at 2 pm?'

*'Sorry. I've got my second cousin's baby's first birthday that day. How
about the week after?'*

. . . and so on and so forth. It's exhausting. Especially if you
times this by three to five close friends.

Now, if you don't have five, three or even one close connection, do not beat yourself up. According to The Friendship
Report, a global study commissioned by Snapchat in 2019, the
average age that we meet our best friend is 21.

Our early twenties is like a second puberty in which we
experience multiple firsts and growth points. We might move
out of home, learn how to change the oil in our car and find
out margaritas are the best, while also learning less-fun lessons
including heartbreak hacks and that waking up for your first
full-time job feels like a full-time job in itself.

It's also a time in life when we have a few more life lessons
under our belt and are more cautious with who we choose to
let enter our lives and befriend.

We can personally vouch for the 21-year statistic as 21 was
the exact age Al was when we met. When we became besties,
though, not *everyone* was thrilled with our union. We were both
in committed relationships with *other* work wives. *Escándalo.*
But, as chance would have it, our work wives both left for six
weeks overseas, leaving us to our own devices. It was during
this time that we transitioned from workmates to soul sisters.
We caught up one-on-one for the first time, and it only took
one question for us to make this transition: 'Do you want to get
a coffee?' The coffee date is a stereotype for a reason. It works!
Honestly, we owe iced lattes so much at this point.

From there, getting to know each other felt easy. The green flags continued to show themselves through common interests as well as contrasting opinions that led to interesting conversations. Most importantly, we genuinely enjoyed each other's company because it felt so natural.

By the time our work wives got back, we had our first of five sets of matching tattoos, a smorgasbord of memories and the ability to communicate telepathically. They weren't exactly thrilled by the realisation that, in their eyes, they'd been replaced. We can totally understand how it must have felt, but we didn't go into the six weeks looking to fill a gap in our social calendar. It just happened. In the end there was also no dramatic fallout with our work wives; we're all still friends to this day, actually, just in a different capacity.

If you're older than 21 and still haven't met your platonic soulmate, don't stress. Life has so many changing factors that you never quite know what it will throw at you, or when. Some of us don't meet a person and say, 'Yep, done. You're my person for life'—and that's okay. Life isn't a Hallmark card, and we all need to stop beating ourselves up for it.

Changing tracks in friendship

Adult friendships are constantly changing alongside whatever whirlwind you're wrapped up in at the time. There are key moments in life—such as when you leave high school, get your first full-time job, fall in love with a romantic partner or move overseas—that shape your friendships. We call these moments track-change events.

A train will be chugging along a particular track, but then someone pulls a lever and it suddenly switches direction. It's still the same train but it is now on a different journey heading towards a new destination.

The same thing happens in adult friendships. Even though we're still the same person, these key moments in life determine new priorities for us. For example, when you're single you might have all the time in the world to see friends. When you get into a romantic relationship, this doesn't change you as a person and your friends might still be a huge priority—but you now have an additional important person in the mix, and your friendships must adjust.

The same can be said when someone takes a gap year overseas or gets their dream job. The life track changes and friendships shift, too. These track-change events don't devalue friendships or make you a bad friend, but they do mean the friendship must adjust.

Sometimes a track-change event can cause the green-eyed monster to rear her naughty head. As a duo, we've been incredibly lucky to share a lot of milestone moments together. We shared our first trip to New York, cried during the rendition of 'For Good' in the *Wicked* Broadway musical, and played mermaids in the crystal-blue waters of Waikiki. Hell, we launched a bloody Spotify Top Five podcast together. While most of our friends and loved ones have been extremely supportive of the success we've shared through our work life slash friendship, we can't say that's the case for everyone. Some people feel left out when we speak our own special language (Grinchlish—*The Grinch* meets English) or tick off bucket-list moments together that we've discussed in other friendships.

We're not blameless victims in this scenario, though. For a while there, it was Sal and Al against the world. There was little to no room for any supporting characters in the feature film that was our friendship. As we've grown and matured together, that has changed. Don't get us wrong—it's still Sal and Al against the world, baby. But we've slowly (and maybe a little reluctantly) loosened our loving stranglehold on each other to make room for other friendships, relationships and passions to flourish.

This was not easy. At the beginning of our friendship, we would literally work our nine to five, go to the gym, text the whole way home then proceed to Instagram DM, Snapchat and continue to text the entire evening.

Wtf.

While we look back on it fondly, this type of fervent friendship is obviously not sustainable—and that's okay. Just like in romantic relationships, we can experience a honeymoon phase in friendships, too. In fact, we believe there are five phases of adult friendships.

The five phases of adult friendships

Let's dissect the five phases commonly experienced when making friends as an adult—Sal and Al scientifically proven.

The 'vibe check' phase

This first phase, aka the curiosity phase, is exactly as it sounds. It's when you find yourself in the same environment as someone and you're both testing the waters to see if you're compatible. Maybe it's in the work kitchen (like us), at a gym class or with your local barista whom you have great banter with every morning. In this phase you find yourself trying to find more opportunities and things to talk about with the person to get a better understanding of their energy.

(Note: we also like to call this 'friendly flirting' but that's probably just 'cos we love to flirt with our friends.)

Not all people you meet pass your vibe check, or maybe you don't pass theirs, and this is completely okay. Just like how you don't fall in love with every date, you won't vibe with every potential friend you meet.

When you know yourself well, you become a skilled master at the vibe check. You'll feel more confident saying, 'What's your Instagram?', 'Let's grab a wine!' or 'Did you want to grab a coffee after our next class?'

Don't be scared of wanting to progress to the next phase, because the high chance is that if you're vibing, they are too!

The 'did we just become best friends?' phase

This phase, aka the honeymoon phase, is obviously lots of fun. The honeymoon phase of friendship is one to let yourself fall into completely. Getting to know someone is *fun*. It's incredibly exciting making a new friend. You get to learn about all the things you have in common, enjoy doing fun things together and make memories that are probably best left out of a wedding speech.

During this phase, your new friend is your favourite person on the planet. In your eyes, every joke is chef's kiss and every weekend involves seeing each other. To put it simply, you're obsessed. In this phase you can sometimes put on the blinders and forget about some of your other friendships. We're not recommending this, but it is a reality that happens in this phase of a new relationship.

The 'warts and all' phase

This phase, aka the teething phase, is one that a lot of friendships don't make it past. After spending as much time as possible with your friend in the honeymoon phase, you'll start to notice some things irk you a little about them. They'll say something that hurts your feelings or they'll get back with the ex who makes you want to take up voodoo.

This phase is so incredibly important for building connections. Your friends aren't perfect—nor can you expect them to be. They might have annoying little tendencies such as always running late or getting a bit rowdy after a few beverages, but they're still your friend regardless.

This is also the phase for more vulnerability, where we open up on a deeper level to talk about our feelings, our insecurities and the things we need from the friendship. This is another reason why some friendships don't make it past this phase— because one or both friends are scared to open up. However, true friendships only happen when you are vulnerable with each other and love each other warts and all, despite your annoying habits.

The 'we can sit in silence and it's not awkward' phase

Being able to sit with your friend in comfortable silence—whether it's in the back of an Uber or lying side by side while you each scroll through TikTok—should be its own official love language (as we mention in Chapter 3).

In this phase, aka the comfortable phase, you no longer feel the need to fill the space. Not talking doesn't mean something is wrong; in fact, it's the complete opposite. You're so comfortable together that you can basically communicate telepathically.

The 'I like you because, I love you despite' phase

The final phase, and the best, is when you reach true understanding and acceptance. You see your friend for everything they are and everything they aren't and wouldn't change a single thing about them. By the time you reach this phase you've likely had a few disagreements. It's these moments that determine whether a friendship is worth it. Does the good outweigh the bad? Sometimes it doesn't, and knowing when to give your friend space or even walk away from a friendship is important.

However, having a friend like this, when you truly see them for all they are and they're still your best friend, is beautiful, empowering and soul fulfilling. You like them for all their incredible qualities and you love them despite some of the imperfections that simply make them human.

The hard truth about friendship

Here's something that might be hard to hear: not everyone you want to be friends with will want to be your friend. Ouch, right?

Nobody likes being rejected—whether it's a job application, a Hinge match or your morning barista telling you they're out of everything bagels.

In *Sex and the City*, an iconic monologue from Miranda gave birth to the now well-known Cab Light Theory. Miranda discusses this theory in relation to heterosexual dating but in our opinion it applies to all relationships, friendships included.

In a nutshell, Cab Light Theory states that when someone is available for a relationship they turn their cab light on. When they don't want a relationship their cab light is off. She goes on to explain that the day they decide to turn their cab light (read: emotional availability indicator) on is when they decide they're ready to settle down, and the next girl they meet will become 'the one' out of sheer dumb luck. Obviously that last part is kind of bullshit, but we think there is an element of truth to this theory.

Not everyone is emotionally available at all times. Some people already have a full cab, and don't have capacity to act on the arm you've stretched out to hail your next great platonic love. So even though you may be ready for a new friendship, that doesn't mean everyone you meet is. Every individual's priorities ebb and flow as life goes on, meaning that making new connections might not be at the top of their to-do list.

If someone doesn't want to be your friend, it often has nothing to do with you. You're not annoying or a crappy human who smells bad like the voice in your head tells you. Their cab light might simply be off.

Once you start approaching making new friends as an adult with this theory in mind, the idea of putting yourself out there becomes less scary and the fear of rejection greatly lessens. The fact that another person isn't picking up what you're putting down won't keep you up till 3 am wondering if you had something in your teeth.

It also means you can focus on the people who have their cab light on, their door open, or whatever metaphorical terminology you want to use that means they're open to new friendships too.

Finding *these* people is the key to finding *your* people.

Life lessons from our chicks

Real-life wisdom fresh from our DMs

Don't force it! Make peace that some people don't want to be close with you. You don't have to be friends with everyone and it doesn't mean that you're unworthy of friendship overall.

How to find new friends

Making friends as an adult is a process of seeking out new-to-you people, then nurturing those connections so they bloom into friendship. But before you even start looking, the first step is to get into the right mindset.

The attitude you hold towards yourself is a big factor in attracting the right kinds of people, which is why being your own best friend is critically important (and why we devoted the entire first chapter to this topic). The attitude you hold towards life as a whole is equally powerful. When you feel joy in everyday life and already live richly in your day to day, that becomes intoxicating to others around you.

We've also learned a lesson from everyone's favourite childhood author, Roald Dahl. In what we believe to be one of his best books, *The Twits*, the antagonist characters are ugly on the outside because they have ugly thoughts on the inside. The lesson being: the more you think ugly thoughts, the uglier you will become.

When we flip this on its head and start to approach life with brightness, we become more attractive—not in an appearance sense, but in an energetic way that will quite literally *attract* people towards us, like we're a magnet.

Put simply, no one likes hanging out with a whinger.

Once you have your mindset sorted, it's time to move to the next step: finding potential connections. Waiting for new friends to find you isn't always the best approach. Sure, sometimes the whole 'it happens when you least expect it' thing can occur. Let's be honest, though: it's a passive approach, and making friends as an adult is best handled as a proactive endeavour. Taking initiative, as intimidating as it may be, is going to lead you to some incredible experiences in life!

To help give you a nudge in the right direction, here are some of the best methods we've found to find new friends in adulthood.

Find common ground

It sounds simple, but finding common ground with someone is an easy place to start developing a friendship. Friendships don't always need to be built off common interests, but it is one of the easiest ways to make new connections. Using your energy to do things you already enjoy doing will have a flow-on effect to finding others who are like-minded. Start by focusing on activities, such as a Run Club, art class or acai at your fave cafe, that are part of your personal rituals, and be open to those you meet there.

Turn co-workers into outside-of-work mates

We're physical proof that the people we meet at work can become friends for life.

When you think about it, the dynamic for connection at work is quite similar to school. Just like school there is forced proximity. If you work in an office from 9 to 5 Monday to Friday every week, you might find yourself becoming friends with people you wouldn't usually cross paths with otherwise. If you're open to it, work can be an incredible way to meet and socialise with people who have completely different experiences and perspectives to your own, yet share a common experience.

Your workplace can also be one of the biggest sources of stress in your life. According to a study conducted in 2023 by Compare the Market, work is the second-highest cause of stress for Australians (personal finances took out the number-one spot). The same study found that 44 per cent of Aussies are stressed by work. That's why a genuine friend in the workplace can be an absolute lifesaver.

Sometimes you don't want to vent to your outside-of-work friends or partner about workplace dramas. Firstly, it can be easier to achieve work-life balance by leaving work drama where it belongs—at work. Plus, the other people in your life probably won't quite understand your frustrations about Suzie from accounting the way your work friend will. While your significant partner or friend can empathise, your work friend understands on a whole different level.

We can't count how many times we've given a workmate a knowing glance as a signal to head out to grab a coffee followed by a brisk walk around the block to blow off steam. It's weird to think that some of our biggest confidantes in life can be found by the water cooler, but it's also pretty fucking cool.

Your work friends don't have to be reserved as a sounding board for work-related bitching, of course. They can also be a source of giggles and reprieve throughout the workday. Whether you're eating lunch together, heading to the gym after work or grabbing drinks at a nearby bar on a Friday arvo, these interactions can act as stepping stones leading to genuine friendship.

In addition to our own friendship, we have been so lucky to connect with many colleagues in a way that transcends the office walls. Over time, some of our friendships went from office coffee runs to slumber parties, wild nights out, road trips and too many personal jokes to count. We've shared moments of celebration such as weddings and birthdays, as well as sadder times such as break-ups, work visa dramas and funerals. It's just like 'real' friendship, because that's exactly what those people became to us.

Workplace friendships can often blossom organically, but it never hurts to be proactive. Invite the new person in the office out for coffee one day. Stay back for Friday drinks. Mingle with different people at the office Christmas party. Who knows, your effort could make the difference between remaining colleagues or becoming friends for life.

A note from Al

Work friends can be part of your best memories and help get you through the worst.

Sal and I have been both super lucky and not so lucky in the manager department. We've had positive experiences—the person who managed us when we left our old job believed in us and supported us to create *Two Broke Chicks*—and some wild rides.

According to an ACAP survey, 3.4 million Australians dislike their manager. Yowza. At one point in our career, we were proud *members of that club of 3.4 million.* We were working close to 12-hour days. We were confused, exhausted and feeling like we weren't good enough at our jobs. Obviously this wasn't true, but that's what you start thinking when you're being managed poorly.

One afternoon we were walking from the office to get hot mochas to try to cheer ourselves up. Sal said to me, 'I can't remember the last time I had a good work week.' I felt the same way.

There were days when we comforted the other as we cried in the bathroom, or talked the other off the ledge of handing in their notice that day. I know it broke Sal's heart (and my own) when I tried to quit, but luckily our work relationship did not end there—otherwise this book wouldn't be here today.

Our friendship with each other, and like-minded colleagues, during this time was a bond forged in the fiery pits of turmoil. If you've also ever disliked your manager or a colleague, you'll get it.

The point is, not every memory you have with your work friends will be of happy times, but these connections can still be deeply meaningful. The support of your colleague friends can get you through the days when you don't have the energy to pick yourself up and dust yourself off.

As wild a time as it was working for that manager, it did give us some great material to look back on and laugh about (even as I write this, I'm sitting next to Sal, chuckling). But all I can say is, thank fuck we work for ourselves now.

Build connections with friends of friends

There's a notion that reaching out to a friend of a friend to hang out is a betrayal. We think this is bullshit. Befriending friends of friends has proven to be one of our most effective strategies to make new friends.

If someone is a friend of a friend, this means your mutual friend has already vetted them as a good person. If you're like-minded and they've passed your friend's vibe check, it's likely you'll get along with them, too.

If you have a mate who always seems to be going to fun social activities, reach out to them and ask if you could come along next time. There's no shame in asking to be included.

A note from Al

I've made most of my closest friends through friends of friends. When I moved away from home I became a Yes Woman. Whenever a friend invited me to a party or beach day I would put my rosé on ice and say, 'Be there with bells on.' It was such an incredible way to grow my social circle.

I've met many long-term friends this way over the years, but my two best friends, Sean and Pia, are two that are very special.

A few years ago I bought a vintage Harley-Davidson shirt off Facebook Marketplace. When I walked into the seller's gorgeous apartment to pick up the shirt, I couldn't help noticing the views across the Vaucluse cliffs, and his stunning girlfriend sitting on the couch. I ended up staying there for 30 minutes chatting to these two people I'd only just met. I remember thinking how weirdly wonderful it was. But, alas, I had a pre-drinks to get to and a bottle of Squealing Pig Rosé with my name on it.

A year later, I was hanging out with some girlfriends who were all invited to a house party. I wasn't invited but they asked if I wanted to come anyway. Since this was my Yes Era of singledom, along I went.

This time I found myself walking into another beautiful apartment overlooking Bondi. It was a far cry from the south Bondi share house I lived in, which had a toilet that would block like a game of Russian roulette.

Everyone was so funny, and I fell into chatting with a couple. They seemed a little familiar but I couldn't place them. Then I noticed the absolutely killer vintage shirt the guy was wearing and it hit me.

'Did you guys ever live in Vaucluse and sell a vintage Harley shirt on Facebook Marketplace?'

Squealing ensued.

Sean, Pia and I were glued together for the rest of the night, and most weekends thereafter.

I admire the warmness and openness Sean and Pia have towards their friends. They're not into cliques and are always the first to dish out an invite. They played a big role in helping me find my people in my twenties. We call them the Mum and Dad of our group, as they're the common denominator between most people in our little gang of misfits.

I also met my now partner and best friend, Rob, through Sean and Pia. One Friday, like so many others, they extended me an invite to drinks at theirs. When I walked in I saw a tall man with blue eyes and dark brown hair. He looked like Damon Salvatore, so it was basically on from that point forward.

There are many other people in my life who I've met through Sean and Pia. Kai, who sings 70 per cent of what she speaks and always makes me smile. Alec, who I'm quite sure has the worst hangovers known to man. Tom, who should never be let near a dance floor. Paul, who never fails to ask how his friends are going and genuinely wants to know. Lucy, who I'm pretty sure is sunshine in human form. There are many others who I love like family. Together we've shared Christmases, beach days, trips down the coast, scavenger hunts and 2 am D&Ms.

These little weirdos have become my people. Sometimes I wish I could go back to my 16-year-old self and tell her, 'It's okay, they're coming, and I promise they're worth waiting for.'

All because I bought a Harley-Davidson shirt off some random guy on Facebook Marketplace.

Try out a friendship app

If we're using apps to find romantic dates, why can't we use them for mate dates too?

Bumble launched its standalone friendship app, Bumble BFF, in 2023. One of our best friends successfully used the app when she moved to New Zealand, so we reckon there's no harm in giving it a go!

Find unity in pain at a workout class

We're not the type to go to a workout class with a pep in our step. For us it's more like dragging our feet, regretting that second serving of mashed potato that's now sitting like a cement block in our belly.

Pre-pandemic we used to go to the gym together, but during lockdown, working from home and the trauma that was 2020, we were no longer in the city together and gym dates became more difficult to organise.

After that, Al got into Pilates but was always a little nervous before class knowing she'd be without her wingwoman. Then one morning she turned to the person on the reformer next to her and started chatting. It was small talk at first, but after a while they were giggling together and exchanging details so they could book into the same class next time.

Finding workout buddies is a great way to double down on those post-workout endorphins, too.

Reach out to old friends

Just because you haven't spoken to someone since high school doesn't mean you can't reach out now. Sometimes friendships can wane over time but can be revived, or you might discover that someone you knew growing up just moved back to your city. Reach out!

It's such a simple hack because you already have the foundation of knowing each other, so it doesn't take as much effort to get things off the ground.

Turn online friendships into IRL ones

When you scroll through your follower list on Instagram, how many people are you actually friends with IRL? If you're anything like us you are probably following quite a few people who are strangers IRL, yet you both double-tap each other's content. Perhaps you have mutual friends, similar interests or live in the same city as this person and that's why you've formed an online friendship of sorts. Regardless of the situation, why not take the leap to move the relationship offline?

It's not considered weird to slide into a potential romantic fling's DMs, so it shouldn't be weird to do the same for a potential friend. Ask them out for a coffee, to catch a movie or to a local gig if you're into the same music. Whatever the scenario, you know you already have something in common with this person, so why not put yourself out there? The worst that could happen is they leave you on read. The best that could happen is you make a new friend. Sounds like pretty good odds to us.

Of course, it's important to put your safety first (sorry to sound like Healthy Harold). If you're planning to meet up in person with someone you only know online, do a little stalk of their followers and tagged photos to see if you spot anything suss. You could also jump on a call or FaceTime beforehand to make sure you're not recreating your own episode of MTV's *Catfish*. If you do decide to catch up, organise to meet them in a public place, tell others where you're going (even better, share your location) and consider inviting someone else to join you for your initial catch-up. It may sound a little over-cautious, but it's always better to be safe than sorry.

A note from Sal

Growing up as a little emo babby who spent many of her teenage years socialising via MSN Messenger and Myspace, I've never thought making friends online was strange. In fact, I met Chris, my partner of now 16 years, through Myspace. We both lived on the South Coast of New South Wales and had mutual friends in real life, so perhaps we would've crossed paths eventually. He initially sent me a friend request because a mutual friend sent him my profile, thinking he'd reckon I was cute.

I still have amazing friendships with some of the people I met on Myspace and bonded with over our mutual love of My Chemical Romance. We've even travelled interstate to meet up, catch a gig or celebrate milestone moments such as weddings together. Because our relationships are defined by mutual passions rather than proximity, many of these friendships that started online have proven to be some of the most meaningful of all.

While I was probably a little more brave (or shameless) about making friends online as a teen, I've also found it a really useful way to make friends as an adult. Aside from my sister and a handful of pals, there aren't many people my age who share my love for eighties heavy metal and rock'n'roll. The Instagram algorithm has worked wonders in connecting me with other people with similar interests. By liking their posts and eventually meeting up for a drink, I've made quite a few friends online as an adult.

Confessing that we've connected with someone online can admittedly feel a bit cringe. But I say, fuck that. If you've made a genuine friendship, that's a win. Who cares how it came about!

Meet friends through hobbies and habits

Making friends through hobbies and habits is a surefire path to success, because you already know you have similar interests or lifestyles. If you're stuck for ideas, here are a few places where you could stumble across folks who are your vibe:

- attend a pottery class
- try a new workout class (Pilates anyone?)
- join a book club
- grab a solo drink at your local bar
- hang out at your local cafe
- watch a sunrise/sunset at your local park
- join a local sports team
- attend a local friendship mixer or meet-up event.

A note from Al

Without sounding too impressed with myself, I do think I'm somewhat of a professional at making friends as an adult. Most of my closest friendships have been forged in my early to mid-twenties.

When I moved away from my local area, separating from high school friends and breaking up with my ex, I was so open to new friendships it wasn't even funny. I basically had a tattoo on my forehead that screamed, 'Wanna be life companions?!'

After living in an apartment with a housemate who barely left their room, I moved into a more social house and met one of my now best friends. We clicked, and to this day I'm convinced we'll get side-by-side tombstones.

Moving into this house was like entering a completely new era. I was starting fresh. I was single in a new suburb and I was ready to *live it up*.

I know it's easy to say, 'Just go out and you'll meet people,' but honestly, as scary as that sounds, it really can be that simple.

During the first week of my new era I was supposed to be heading out on a Hinge date. My new housemate, Sidnee, was encouraging me to get out there with no expectations. Just rip off the bandaid of sorts.

The date was a mess. In fact, it didn't even happen.

The first red flag was that it was on a hill. That's it: the plan was just to sit on the side of a hill. The second red flag was when I asked if we should pick up food, and they replied they had 'already eaten'. The third was that when I got there at the agreed-upon time they were running 'an hour-ish late'.

Fuck that.

Feeling a little defeated I started walking home, and on the way passed an absolute vibe of a rock'n'roll bar. Never in my life had I gone and sat in a bar on my own, but I was committed to turning the night around.

Fast forward an hour and I was best friends with the two bartenders, Bron and Kip, who had heard all about the date that never happened. Then Sidnee walked past with a bag of carrots.

I can't quite put into words how strange it was seeing this girl I'd known for about a month, in the doorway of a bar, waving around a bag of carrots. She was screaming, 'Why aren't you on your date?!' Carrots were flying through the air.

When I filled her in she promptly sat down with me and ordered herself a drink.

The next three hours were spent with Sidnee, Bron, Kip and our carrots, hanging out and talking smack. It was a night in which I didn't intend to make new friends, but I'd just had my first drinks with my housemate and soon-to-be best friend, and made two new ones in Bron and Kip. We went on to spend many evenings together, and I can also no longer even look at a tequila shot thanks to those two.

It was on that night that I developed my favourite phrase to say to a new friend: 'I've decided. Can I force my friendship on you?'

It's cheesy and always said with a laugh, and it works. This phrase helped me become best friends with a gym trainer, a hair stylist, my Pilates neighbour, a massage therapist and many more who have become some of my closest friends.

Making friends as an adult is about putting yourself out there. Obviously you can't just pull out a cheesy line and, boom, you've got a new bestie, but you do need to let them know you're interested in spending more time with them.

Not once after saying this phrase has anyone ever screamed for help, run away or looked at me like I had three heads. Nothing bad is going to happen if you tell someone you want to be mates with them.

The moment you stop overthinking what other people are thinking about you, you free yourself of fear and anxiety. You shut down that little voice that says, 'But what if they don't want to be friends with me?' It's like water off a duck's back.

There are times when I've used my line and no friendship has been born out of it. But more often than not, a new connection has sparked. I don't stay awake at night staring at the ceiling stressing about all the times the phrase didn't work, because I genuinely can't even remember them.

I *can* remember the friendships that exist to this day, though.

Opening a door to building friendship can be scary, and requires you to let go of the fear of rejection. However, it is the first of many stepping stones to making friends as an adult.

How to build a friendship

Once you've started a conversation, found some common interests or felt they just had the best vibe ever, it's time to get proactive.

There are two things that build friendships as an adult: consistency and vulnerability. These two things can be very hard—especially considering two things that get in the way of friendship is lack of time and trust.

We've probably all experienced meeting a new person, vibing with them and finishing the chat with the 'we should hang out sometime' sign-off while waving, albeit a little awkwardly, and backing towards our car/bus/flying horse. So *why* do we never actually 'hang out sometime'?

It's because, when it comes to crunch time, we feel too nervous to initiate the conversation and put ourselves out there to face possible rejection.

Leave this at the door. Right now.

Because making friends as an adult means sending that follow-up message. It means saying, 'Can I get your number or Instagram? I'd love to hang out sometime' *before* you awkwardly wave while doing the moonwalk to your flying car.

It also means not waiting two months to finally get the guts to message them. Initiative matters. You can't wait for them to message you declaring their undying need for your friendship—they're very likely just as nervous as you are to send the first text. Stripping back society's weird obsession with heterosexual relationship language, you're basically asking this person on a date. A platonic date. Of course that's going to make you feel a bit squiggly in the tummy.

In these moments it's best to remind yourself of one of our favourite life lessons in the entire universe: *if nothing changes, nothing changes.*

If you don't put yourself out there, you'll be exactly where you are now, and this new person you vibed with is probably not going to become a future friend. So if you say 'We should catch up sometime!' be consistent with your word and actually reach out to make it happen.

However, if you are brave enough to get vulnerable, you shift the scales to change your environment. If they say no, you've still achieved something you were scared of doing. If they say yes, tada! We've got a friendship date. Yee-haw!

Once said friendship date has finally come to fruition, make sure to follow up if you had a good time. Let's say you picked the restaurant for the first catch-up, shoot them a text and say it's their turn and you'd love to check out one of their favourite spots. Especially when a friendship is in its early days, you need to put in that little bit of extra effort to make sure it flourishes.

Dear Sal and Al

I feel like I can't keep friends in my life. The friendship fizzles, they make new friends or we have a falling-out. I'm starting to feel like I'm the problem. I don't know why it's so hard to keep people in my life. What am I doing wrong?

Hey chick,

First of all, know that making, keeping and sustaining friendships can be *really* hard. Life throws so many curveballs that it can feel like a juggling act to keep them all in the air. Difficulty in maintaining friendships is a very common problem a lot of people experience in their life.

The good news is, you're already one step ahead. Looking inward and assessing how you may contribute to friendships coming and going is practising a level of awareness that some can find uncomfortable. It's a much easier option to lean into blissful ignorance and think we did nothing wrong. Being honest with ourselves, truly honest, is never easy—but it's integral to holding on to friendships.

A lot of the time, when we see multiple relationships falling through, there is a common thread. This may be to do with your attachment style.

Your attachment style determines your ability to build and commit to strong and consistent relationships (including friendships). Dr Courtney Conley, therapist, author and professor, says, 'At its simplest level, attachment is an emotional bond with another person.'

There are four different attachment styles: avoidant, anxious, disorganised and secure. To understand where you sit, you do need to be honest—but by the sounds of it, you're already committed to understanding yourself more fully.

Avoidant attachment (aka dismissive)

The avoidant attachment style means you may pride yourself on being a bit too independent. Being vulnerable, talking about your feelings and getting close to someone is your idea of nightmare fuel.

This style tends to be so wary of being close to someone they avoid it all together.

Signs this may be you:

⊛ When someone tries to get close to you, you pull away or 'get the ick'.

⚜ You're uncomfortable talking about your own and others' emotions.

⚜ You believe it's better to rely on yourself completely than anyone else.

⚜ When you feel hurt, you find it easy to detach and begin declining plans and not responding to this person anymore.

While you may think you can take the world on by yourself, as humans one of our most fundamental needs is connection. There is such a thing as being healthily self-sufficient, but this attachment style is more a form of self-preservation arising from a fear of being hurt. Your distanced emotions can make your friends feel as though they're not important to you.

An improved approach to friendships:

Just like no one best friend can serve all your needs, neither can you. We need human interaction and connection to evolve into the best versions of ourselves. Yes, trusting someone else whether it's a romantic or platonic relationship is scary, but that doesn't mean you won't be okay.

Give yourself permission to be deserving of friendship.

Anxious attachment (aka preoccupied)

This attachment style is normally related to our self-esteem and is basically the opposite of the avoidant style. People with an anxious attachment style may feel needy or clingy in their relationships (platonic and romantic). The person with this style tends to need constant reassurance from others in their lives.

Signs this may be you:

- You find yourself jealous when your friends or partner spend time with other people.
- You find yourself over-apologising for small things.
- Your self-worth depends on how your friends feel about you and how much time they spend with you.
- You feel anxious when spending time alone.

An improved approach to friendships:

This style can have you listening to an internal narrative that isn't true. When your friend can't hang out because they're busy, they might actually just be busy. But you convince yourself that people are going to leave you, so you unconsciously start pushing them to do so by holding on to them too tightly.

In those moments you want to grasp on to your friendships, challenge the way you're thinking and feeling.

Is there any evidence as to why this person wouldn't want to be your friend anymore? Likely not.

Does hanging out with other people mean they've randomly decided they don't like you? No.

Disorganised attachment (aka disoriented)

This style often feels undeserving of connection and believes that they are unworthy of friendship. If this is you, you may find it difficult to manage your emotions and self-soothe. This style often goes up and down in their friendships. One second they're obsessed with the friendship and the next they're cutting that person off.

Signs this may be you:

⊛ Your disposition towards your friend changes quickly and often between love and hate.

⊛ You don't think you're 'good enough' for others' friendship.

⊛ You can find being open and intimate with people confusing, and it may cause you to shut down.

An improved approach to friendships:

This attachment style can incorporate traits from both anxious and avoidant styles. Try to reflect on which traits feel most familiar to you in order to understand where they stem from. The main point though is that you do *want* to form connections, so lean into this. Start easy and don't push yourself. Begin with understanding your boundaries and healing through talking to someone you trust.

Secure attachment

Secure attachment is looked on very positively and deemed the 'healthiest' of all attachment styles, but there are still some traits that can impact your friendships negatively. This attachment style often feels very comfortable building connections with others and doesn't feel intimidated by being open, nor insecure about feelings not being returned.

However, being secure means you may not notice when your friends display different attachment styles. Because you don't need reassurance, you may not notice an anxious attachment style friend who does. When an avoidant friend is receding back into their shell, you may just believe them to be 'doing their own thing'.

To put it in simple terms:

Knowing your attachment style helps you to understand the 'why' behind some of your actions. It can help you talk to yourself and get to the bottom of how you're feeling and why you do some things.

That said, there is no one size fits all to friendship; every connection we have as humans runs on its own track, and we can't be prepared for every track change along the way. Don't try to over-analyse every decision you make. It's good to be self-aware and understand your emotions and why some friendships turn out the way we do, but becoming *too* self-reflective can make you fearful of making any decision at all!

If you think you may relate to one or more of these attachment styles and it feels overwhelming, we definitely recommend speaking to someone qualified who can give you more specific tools to work with your attachment style.

In the meantime, feel safe with the thought that not everyone immediately 'clicks'. True friends can take time to find, but we promise they are out there.

Lots of love,

Sal and Al

Adult friendship life lessons

Okay, you're now officially ready to meet your people. We've given you a lot to work with in this chapter. But if you're going into a situation where you could potentially make a new friend and get overwhelmed, here are thirteen life lessons that'll serve you well:

① Go in with the expectation people will like you.
② Don't take rejection personally.
③ Realise that the worst-case scenario isn't really that bad.
④ Believe you can find new friendships anywhere.
⑤ Understand there's no such thing as a perfect friendship.
⑥ Don't be passive—it's up to you to get the ball rolling.
⑦ Smile. Enjoy yourself.
⑧ Be yourself.
⑨ Put down your phone.
⑩ Listen to understand, not to respond.
⑪ Give compliments.
⑫ Show an interest in their passions.
⑬ If you're vibing with someone, get vulnerable and tell them you want to be friends.

A note from Sal

During the process of writing this book, I turned 30.

I know. I appreciate your condolences.

I felt somewhat prepared after witnessing some of my close friends enter their thirties before me. Yet going on how people talk about aging from twenty-something to thirty-something, part of me was expecting a massive transformation. I thought maybe I'd wake up at 12.01 am on the day of my 30th birthday as a whole new woman who was more mature, responsible and wise than the version I fell asleep as. I thought my relationships would magically transfigure as well. Watching *Suddenly 30* every year since 2004 probably didn't help me gain a realistic vision of my thirties, either.

I'm not sure if this is normal for a 30-year-old or a result of the pandemic pause, but I don't feel *that* different to how I felt in my late twenties. Neither do my friendships. But when I look back, I suppose a lot has evolved. In a stereotypical contradiction, it feels like nothing yet *everything* has changed in the last decade.

In the nicest way possible, I feel like I expect less from my friendships now. I value my friends more than ever, but I don't rely on them with the same intensity as I did in my early twenties. I have more patience when it takes my friends a few days to text back. I'm gentler in the way I give tough love. I try to take a more diplomatic approach to how I deal with conflict. I don't take it personally when a friend has to bail on plans and, instead, use it as a good excuse to spend some quality time alone. Maybe I'm softening in my 'old age'.

In my early twenties, I considered 30 to be geriatric and expected most of my friends to be married with children by now. As the typical young Millennial experience would have it, though, most of my friends haven't gotten married or started having kids yet. But it is *starting* to happen, and I can see how individual friends entering different phases in their lives can dramatically change a friendship.

For example, my older sister and best friend since birth Meg recently had her first baby: a little girl who I am *obsessed* with. Even though we live 90 minutes apart, my sister and I used to spend most days DMing across multiple platforms and spend every second weekend together. Our calendars were always peppered with upcoming concerts, slumber parties, nights out and vintage shopping dates. However, her life and priorities have obviously changed massively since giving birth, and I can no longer expect her to drop everything just because I feel like having a sleepover.

While part of me is sad that the old chapter of our friendship is now closed, it *is* a small part that's easily overshadowed by the positives. The overwhelming silver lining of this is that it is an absolute privilege to watch my beautiful sister step into her new chapter of motherhood. It's also incredible to know a new, wonderful friendship is ready to blossom with my beautiful niece Maeve and the memories we're all yet to share.

As my other friends' lives change—whether it's getting more invested in serious relationships or focusing on their careers—I expect that a similar pattern will continue to emerge. Not even a year into my third decade, though, I understand there is plenty of room for these friendships to continue to evolve.

I do look back on the nature of my friendships in my early twenties with some nostalgia. I miss the wild house parties that would host some of our best-ever stories. The ability to drop everything on a random Tuesday night to head to the movies with friends. Late-night Maccas runs and weekend brunches giggling about first dates gone wrong.

However, friendship in my thirties is just as beautiful in its own way. The friendships in my life feel more secure. Old relationships are bound by a rich history and new ones are founded on mutual interests rather than out of fleeting convenience. While some of the friendships may look different now, it feels like an honour to witness my mates growing up into the incredible people they were destined to be.

IT'S NOT ALWAYS DAISIES, SPARKLES AND UNICORN FARTS

05.

Friendship is one of the most beautiful, magical and rewarding experiences in life. It can also be heartbreaking, awkward and tricky to navigate. Even the strongest friendships will likely involve some awkward pauses, hiccups and the occasional cold shoulder.

Navigating tension, conflict or disagreements and apologising to a friend is a fine art of diplomacy. It's always going to be a little bit awkward, but by the end of this chapter you'll be an absolute pro at managing glitches in your friendships and hopefully feel less pressure to make your friendships perfect.

Five friendship myths we don't vibe with

Relationships are temporary, friendship is forever. You are the company that you keep. By chance we met, by choice we became friends. There are many quotes, rules and commandments about friendship that we agree with. However, there are some that we don't believe. So let's bust some of the myths you've heard about friendship.

1. Don't ever move in with a friend

Before moving out of home for the first time, we both heeded the warning: don't move in with a friend! Whenever we ask our chicks to share their biggest life lessons learned from moving out of home, we always receive the same caution. While this can be a valid piece of advice, it's not always true. We have both been lucky enough to have amazing experiences living with good friends. If you're really close, it can feel like one big slumber party and makes everyday activities such as cooking dinner, grabbing groceries and midweek reality TV binges way more fun.

What we will say is that you should only move in with the *right* type of friend. In our case, we've known beforehand that we were very compatible with the friends we moved in with. If you're a clean freak and your friend hasn't quite grasped the concept of how to get the dishes from the sink into the dishwasher, you may run into trouble. The same goes if you have totally different lifestyles. A differing lifestyle might not matter too much when you're not living together, but it can cause clashes if you're housemates. For example, if your friend is a shift worker who goes to bed early during the week and you're a social butterfly who wants to invite people over midweek, we predict some awkward convos in your future.

It is important to note that even if you are the most perfect match as roommates and you're simply obsessed with each other as friends, you're going to annoy each other at some point and potentially have a few spats. It could be over something as little as taking out the garbage. When you're in each other's space constantly, there are going to be moments of differing opinions and habits. That's life.

Overall, though, some of our favourite memories from our twenties are from when we lived with friends. While approaching living with a friend with caution is smart, you could miss out on making some amazing memories if you make 'don't live with friends' a hard-and-fast rule to live by.

2. Friendship tattoos are the kiss of death

Well, this is awkward. We've all heard that getting a matching or tribute tattoo for a loved one is like the kiss of death. Curse or no curse, we're both partial to a matching tattoo. We got our first matching tattoos (basic roses, but we love them) within a few months of knowing each other. Almost seven years later, we now have five sets of matching tattoos, with more likely to come. Including the ones she shares with Al, nine out of ten of Sal's tattoos are matching with a friend or family member. None of these relationships have succumbed to the supposed tattoo curse as of yet.

Personally, we just don't think it's that deep. Even if you don't stay friends with someone you have a matching tattoo with, you can still look back on the memories fondly. If things end badly, you can always get it covered up or use it as a reminder of the life lesson you picked up from the experience. As long as it's not offensive, we say go get that ink, baby!

3. Straight men and women can't be 'just friends'

It's the question that fuelled the plot of the 1989 rom-com *When Harry Met Sally*: can straight men and women really be friends with zero romance? Yes, we're aware that this sounds like a myth believed by primary school children or your jealous ex, and it's the epitome of heteronormativity. But apparently it's a cause of contention that's on quite a few people's minds.

A 2019 study published in the *Journal of Relationships Research* found that people who are sceptical of straight male–female friendships are more likely to 'lash out' when they feel threatened by their partner's friend, rather than communicating with their partner or the friend. Shocker.

We've both had many male friends. In fact, some of our best friends are straight men with whom we've never had anything but platonic relationships. In our opinion, restricting yourself to friendships with people of a gender you wouldn't typically be attracted to is *extremely* limiting. Also, how does this rule apply to non-binary, bisexual and pansexual pals? It doesn't. Because it's stupid.

If your partner is displeased that you're friends with someone they think you could be attracted to, that's a projection of their insecurities.

4. Friendship should never be boring

Friendships can't always be wild nights out, piping-hot gossip or massive giggle sessions. You know when you have just got back to your hotel room at 4 pm and lie next to each other in silence while you take part in a solo activity such as reading a book or playing on your phone? Our friend Hannah Ferguson (Cheek Media co-founder and all-round bad-arse) calls that 'cage time' and it's literally the best. Boring, but the best.

5. Friends never make you feel left out

At some point in our lives, we've all felt left out. We're not talking about when you were the last person to race to the swings in kindy or when your teacher said 'pair up' and you looked around in a panic because you didn't have a partner. We're talking about when you're an adult, and you experience moments when you feel like you're being left behind. This can happen when you don't have plans but it seems everyone occupying your Instagram Stories does, or you see two friends hanging out but you weren't invited.

Being left out triggers the very human fear of rejection. When we feel left out, we automatically think people are moving on without us when, most of the time, that is very likely not the case. Stop pulling the emergency alarm and going into an emotional bunker.

Yes, sometimes friends will hang out and you won't be invited.

No, this doesn't mean they've woken up, made their coffee and decided you're their mortal enemy. If it's a one-off Saturday brunch that didn't make it to your message inbox, it's probably nothing to overthink about.

That said, if you're feeling left out *all* the time that's cause for thought. It might be an opportunity to reevaluate some of the friendships in your life.

Also remember you don't need to wait for invitations. You can initiate interaction and make plans with your friends, too.

Fighting with your friends

Fighting with your friends fucking sucks, and it's an inevitable fate for most friendships. Most of us don't enjoy putting the metaphorical dukes up with our mates, which is probably why we're really bad at it. Disagreeing with a friend is its own brand of awkward and uncomfortable—even more so than conflicting with a family member or romantic partner.

This is probably why, at least anecdotally, friends are more likely to sweep things under the rug rather than approach them head-on. Unless you've got yourself a magic carpet, the passive-aggressive comments, awkward tension and unpaid dinner bills don't disappear. Instead, they grow and fester with time. This is when they explode into blow-up fights. Sometimes you can overcome these conflicts, but sometimes they can be cataclysmic for the relationship and this can be hard to come back from.

We've found that having the tough convo when the point of conflict is fresh is usually the way to go. Exactly how these conversations go down will also vary from friend to friend. You may need to switch tack depending on whether you're dealing with a straight shooter who is going to tell you exactly how they feel versus a super-sensitive friend who keeps their cards close to their chest. This chapter contains some strategies on how to approach this tricky subject with different types of friends, don't you worry.

Before we get into that, though, it's important to understand that these conversations don't have to be confrontational. You can conduct them calmly, with kindness. Conflict can be a vehicle for both you and your friend to grow. It does involve a great deal of work and empathy to do it well, though, so we'll also run through how to know whether a friendship is *worth* saving or if it's time to let it go.

We're going to tackle this from both sides and give you tips on how to deal with conflict with your mates whether you're in the right, wrong or somewhere in the middle. Because, as Al's mum always says: 'There are three sides to every story. Yours, theirs and the truth.'

When should you bring up a conflict?

You don't have to bring up every single grievance that you have with a friend. This can come across as naggy, overly critical and be an unproductive practice for your friendship.

In our podcast interview with *She's on the Money* host Victoria Devine, she shared an interesting life lesson that can be applied here. It was a piece of advice she picked up from her dad. After venting to him that she was annoyed at some people and situations in her life, he replied, 'Temper honesty with mercy.' Basically, you should weigh up how honest you need to be when you're giving someone feedback. Not all criticism is constructive.

Even if it's coming from a genuine grievance, is it *really* worth potentially hurting your friend's feelings by bringing it up? Also, how much detail do you need to go into to get your point across? You may have all of the read receipts to prove your friend has been shit on the replies, but is it necessary to show them? There may be a kinder and more constructive way to share how you're feeling.

For example, do you need to criticise your friend for having a messy car or a deep love for reality TV? Probably not. Do you need to bring up that they're *always* 20 minutes late when you catch up or suck at paying you back when you go out for drinks together? Yes.

A good rule of thumb when deciding whether to bring up a grievance is determining whether it's hurting you, your friend or anyone else. If the answer is no, this is a time to temper your honesty with mercy.

We were recently asked what the key to our friendship has been. We're genuinely so flattered when we're asked questions like this.

A few years ago, in our early twenties, we would've answered this differently to what we would say now. Years ago, with a twinkle in our eye and a chuckle, we would have said, 'Oh, it's that we're the same person!' We thought our friendship was built on the astronomical number of uniquely shared interests we had. All of our colleagues, friends and acquaintances over the years would joke that we're twins. Even the barista making our morning iced lattes said this.

However, as we've grown older, our answer has changed. It's not our shared interests and personality traits that make our friendship so strong, but our ability to disagree with each other. We tell each other the truth, even if it's hard.

As much as our friends deserve our undying support, they also deserve our unfiltered honesty. As friends we can sometimes assume it isn't our duty to tell our mates hard truths. Leave it to the spouses, family members or colleagues, even—it's easier, right?

The way we see it, who better to tell you something you might not want to hear than someone with absolutely no obligation to be in your life? Your friends aren't married to you or related by blood. They're not a contractually obligated boss who has regulated check-ins to make sure you're performing at the top of your game.

There are a multitude of different opinions on this matter. Some believe that friends aren't there to lecture but to simply support you and be there for you when you need them. Others think that if you're not being brutally honest with each other all the time you're building a friendship based on smoke, mirrors and dishonesty.

To be honest (ha-ha, see what we did there?), neither are correct and both are right.

Good friends are never waiting to catch you out when you take a step wrong. There will be people you meet in life who get a kick out of feeling smarter, funnier and more powerful than you. These people aren't your friends. Friends don't take joy in your misery. They don't jump at the chance to tell you how you're wrong and spend the next 45 minutes explaining how they would have behaved differently. This is toxic, and we'll go into it in more detail in Chapter 6. (Hint: dump them.)

The friends who are there to give you loyal and careful truths are those who will make you a better person. Behind these moments of gentle honesty is the unwavering support that we think sits on a parallel lane. A genuine friend is one who will hold your hand and walk you out of moments of misjudgement and liberate you from some delusions you hold.

If we cannot even trust our friends to tell us the truth about ourselves, what can we trust them with?

If we put things in a 'do not disturb' folder, they never go away. This is true in all relationships. It's like the scene in *Bruce*

Almighty where he tries to sift through prayers by changing their physical form. From filing cabinets to Post-it notes and finally emails, the abundance doesn't disappear but in fact continues to grow.

The thing you leave unsaid starts as a piece of gravel in your shoe and before you know it it's a metaphorical boulder hurtling towards the relationship, ready to inflict some serious damage.

As best friends, we've found the unwavering support quite easy. We're not perfect and we've not always made the right decisions, but who has? We're humans, and a lot of the time we react with emotional knee-jerk responses only to cool down and think . . . oops. One time, during a *very* single period, Al started flirting with the biggest crumb of a human being. Literally an hour later she turned to Sal with horror and exclaimed, 'What was I thinking?!' Sal, always to the emotional rescue, simply said, 'I think you were really tired.'

It was 5 pm.

With every 'I fucked up', 'I made a mistake' or 'I'm not sure I did the right thing' there have been two sure things in our friendship:

① We never judge.
② We tell the truth, even if it's sticky and the other might not necessarily want to hear it.

Our friendship has been built on those moments when we've disagreed or not quite known what to do. We know how to have different opinions, and it isn't the end of the world. Even better, we can respect each other's opinions and listen to what the other has to say, knowing that whatever is said comes from a place of ride-or-die support and love.

Five signs you should bring an issue up with a friend

It can be difficult to know when it is even worth having these types of conversations with friends. We know that it can feel a bit dramatic to pull your friend aside to have a serious chat, especially if it might seem to come out of the blue. Sometimes it feels easier to shrug it away with a vague excuse: 'Oh, that's what our friendship has always been like' or 'We're just drifting, I guess.' If you're unsure whether you should bring up an issue with a friend or let it go, here are five signs that you need to have the tough convo with your mate.

1. You're being passive aggressive

We all have our low moments when we might unintentionally snap at a friend or roll our eyes like a petulant teenager. If this happens occasionally when you've had a particularly shitty day at work or haven't had your full eight hours, that's fair enough. However, if you find yourself frequently responding passive aggressively to your friend, it's time to get it out in the open. You might think that your friend doesn't notice when you side-eye someone else while they're talking or mutter something under your breath, but we assure you, they do. We say this not to scold you, but because we've been guilty of this ourselves. Not only is passive aggression a little mean and immature, it's not going to help you resolve what's going on and is most likely going to sour the relationship.

2. You're bitching to others about your friend

Venting to someone else is *totally* natural and we all need to have a little bitch once in a while. If anything, it can be a super-healthy way to get something off your chest, not to mention the potential perspective or advice you could get from sharing your annoyance with a third party. However, if you find yourself regularly finding ways to bitch about your friend or repeating the same critiques, it's time to bring up your issue with your friend. Nothing positive can come from running your mouth to a bunch of different people. You'd rather your friend hear of your grievances in your own words than courtesy of the grapevine.

3. It's lingering on your mind

In an article on *The Everygirl* on navigating conflict with friends, licensed clinical psychologist Jaime Zuckerman says if some-thing comes up in your mind more than three times a day, it's worth exploring.

As well as Zuckerman's three-times-a-day rule, we'd also posit that if something is still lingering in your mind three days later, it's time to bring it up. That way you've given yourself enough time to avoid attacking your friend in the heat of the moment, but it's hung around long enough in your mind that you know it's an issue worth mentioning.

4. You're avoiding your friend

You might find excuses to avoid spending time with your friend because you don't want to confront them. But these things don't always solve themselves. Even if your annoyance feels less intense over time, it's hard to continue a healthy and solid friendship on a foundation of resentment. Rather than dodging the issue, you're better off putting on your big-person pants and confronting the issue head-on.

5. They're acting differently towards you

Most of the earlier examples apply when you feel that your friend is in the wrong. However, what if you're the one in the wrong? If your friend hasn't confronted you but the vibes are off, if they're not replying to your text messages or acting cold when you're together, you may need to suck it up and ask them if you've done something wrong. You don't need to be accusatory. You can simply say, 'You've seemed a bit down lately, is anything wrong?' or 'I haven't heard from you in a while. Is everything okay?' Fingers crossed that'll give them the gentle prod they need to open up. If you don't get a response, that might be the clearest answer you need.

It also may have nothing to do with you. They may have other things going on in their personal life that are impacting how they're interacting with you. Regardless, it will give them the floor to explain how they're feeling, and will hopefully be the first step to getting your friendship back on track.

How to manage conflict with a friend

There is no rule book on how to have the perfect fight with your friend. Exactly how you deal with your grievances will depend on the root cause of the tiff, your friendship dynamic and your specific personalities. In our experience, though, there are definitely a few do's and don'ts that can help make the process easier and more productive.

Have realistic expectations

Before you even consider *how* to resolve a conflict with a friend, you need to set yourself up with realistic expectations. You can't predict the outcome, but you can try to prepare emotionally for the possible results.

Regardless of who you think is in the wrong or your grand plans to make it up to your friend, they may have a different understanding of the events. You may have hurt your friend more than you realised and they may not be willing to rekindle the friendship. Or they may be unwilling to take responsibility (or incapable of doing so) so that you can move on from what has happened.

You should also be prepared to hear things that may be upsetting, confronting or difficult to take in. This is important to understand before going into it, otherwise you may react defensively instead of taking the opportunity to really listen to your friend.

You should also prepare yourself for how things may eventuate post-conflict. Even if you do resolve things, the friendship may not return to how it once was.

Don't do it over text

Conflict resolution should always happen in person. If your friend lives far away or you can't make time to meet in person, you should at least chat over the phone or a video call. This is because an earnest comment can come across as passive aggressive over a text message. It's really hard to read tone and communicate with the level of detail you may need to. The security of your phone screen may feel more comfortable, but a good friendship that's worth fighting for deserves an IRL setting.

Give your friend a heads up

When you're reaching out to your friend to chat, you may want to give them a heads up on what has been on your mind and what you want to chat about. This can feel awkward, but it's better than blindsiding your friend and can also give them time to reflect before you chat.

Choose your time and place

Make sure you're giving this conversation enough time to unfold as it needs to. It's probably best not to schedule this chat on your lunch break or shortly before you have an appointment booked in. You don't want to have to rush the conversation or cut it short before anything has been resolved. Instead, schedule it when you're both free and have the space to dedicate as much time to the conversation as it needs.

Organise to catch up somewhere that's easy for you both to get to. We suggest somewhere private enough that you can express yourself without feeling awkward about other people eavesdropping on your conversation. We also suggest picking a quiet space where you don't need to awkwardly shout over any background noise to get your point across. Perhaps invite your friend over to your house or, if you'd prefer to chat somewhere in public, grab a coffee and walk to a lookout or park to sit down and chat.

It's best to have this conversation in an alcohol-free zone. While some social lubricant may be tempting, emotions can become more heightened when alcohol is involved. Plus, it may be more difficult for you to remember the points and examples that'll help you articulate how you've been feeling if you've sunk a couple of bevvies.

Wait till you've cooled off

Confronting your friend while you're mid-rage blackout isn't the best idea. When you're swept up in your emotions, you're more likely to say things without a filter. While these things may come from a seed of truth, it may not be the kindest or most practical way to go forward.

If you're feeling upset or betrayed, you may sink to a low verbal blow to get revenge on your friend in the heat of the moment. This could give you a millisecond of vindication, but these heated confrontations can really hurt a friendship in the long run. Instead, give yourself a few days to cool off or at least sleep on it before you have the conversation. This can also help you see past the fog of anger, sadness or betrayal to see your friend's perspective more clearly.

Use 'I' statements rather than 'you' statements

Using 'I' statements can be a respectful and constructive way to resolve conflict with your friends. That's because 'I' statements come across in a less accusatory way than 'you' statements. Using 'I' statements shows that you're taking responsibility for your feelings. Your friend may feel attacked if you lead the conversation with a long list of things they did, instead of balancing this with 'I' statements that bring yourself into the conversation.

Here are some examples of how you can swap 'you' statements for 'I' statements in a tough convo with a friend.

'You' statement	'I' statement
'You never message me and you don't appreciate our friendship.'	'I feel like I'm always the one to send the "let's catch up" message and I feel unappreciated.'
'You always make jokes at my expense and it hurts my feelings.'	'My feelings are hurt when jokes are made at my expense.'
'You always embarrass me in front of our other friends.'	'I felt really embarrassed the other night when this happened.'
'You only hang out with me when you want something.'	'I feel like we only spend time together when I can do something for you.'
'You never tell me how you're feeling.'	'I would love to know how you're feeling.'

Listen to your friend

The point of the conversation isn't to tell your friend how you're feeling and bail. You need to give your friend space to express themselves and share their side of the story. This is really difficult, but you should try not to be defensive or interrupt them as they're speaking. Instead, listen to what they have to say and make mental notes to respond with once they've shared their piece.

It's also important to have some empathy. Your friend is likely going to be upset, defensive, embarrassed or a combination of these emotions and more. In our experience, we've found that when we've had confrontations with friends (whether on the giving or receiving end) one party often doesn't realise the effect their actions have had. We've probably all been the shitty friend at one point or another and sometimes this comes as a result of chaos happening in our own lives. Depending on the scenario, it's important to show your friend some grace, understanding and forgiveness if you want to take steps to repair the friendship.

Take responsibility for your part in the conflict

Fights with friends are almost never one-sided. Even if you feel like you're the one who has been wronged the worst, you probably played your part in how the conflict went down. Take the opportunity to admit the role you played and make any necessary apologies.

A note from Sal

I used to find it really hard to take responsibility and apologise when fighting with friends. As a quintessential Pisces, I admit I've been known to have a bit of a martyr complex. This is something I've actively worked on in my twenties and now thirties.

When I was younger I also found it really hard to forgive people or give them the benefit of the doubt during times of conflict. Instead of taking responsibility for my actions or how I could've contributed to the problem, I'd usually come prepared with a long list of receipts of my friend's wrongdoings and a list of justifications to excuse my often shitty behaviour.

However, I quickly learned this served no one, including myself. Instead, as I've gotten older, I've learned to approach conflict with more softness and give people room to speak without needing to immediately whack a comeback at them.

I've learned that, as long as everyone has aired how they feel and taken accountability for their actions, the more mature and strong move is to both accept and give an apology.

Aim for compromise and solution

Once you've both shared how you feel, the conversation should ideally end with a compromise and plan for how you can move forward. For example, let's say you're always the one reaching out or organising plans. The compromise could be to book in a coffee date every month at an agreed place and time, so the ball isn't always in your court to organise it. Or maybe you can agree to go tit for tat and alternate who picks the location and time for your catch-ups.

If possible, it's best to have an actionable outcome that you can both be held accountable for. If the outcome is a little wishy-washy ('I promise I'll make more of an effort'), your friendship may regress into its old patterns yet again.

Apologise

So you've realised you've fucked up, you're in the wrong and want to say 'I am sorry' to your friend. Yet somehow those three little words feel too hard to say, or they don't feel like they're enough.

Well, you're in luck, because there are scientifically backed strategies on how to make an effective apology. In a 2016 study published in *Negotiation and Conflict Management Research*, the authors found that a good apology must contain these six components:

1. expression of regret
2. explanation of what went wrong
3. acknowledgement of responsibility
4. declaration of repentance
5. offer of repair
6. request for forgiveness.

Another study conducted by Dr Jennifer Thomas and Dr Gary Chapman came up with five apology love languages: expressing regret, accepting responsibility, making restitution, genuinely repenting and requesting forgiveness. According to this study, saying 'I'm wrong and I'm sorry' will reach 77 per cent of people. But apparently the remaining 23 per cent require a little extra TLC, which is where the additional love languages come in.

While these are all key components of a strong apology, the research also takes into account that you need to tailor the apology to the person you're making amends with. Different types of apologies may be required depending on your friend's needs, your friendship dynamic and how badly you dropped the ball.

It's also important to take responsibility for your own emotions. Even when you feel really guilty, you can't expect your friend to manage your feelings. Instead, if you know your actions have really hurt your friend, you need to focus on what you can do to repair the friendship and regain their trust.

The entirety of the apology shouldn't be about offloading how bad you feel in a way that guilts your friend into forgiving you. Not only is this kind of guilt-tripping not fair on your friend, but it's not the most stable foundation for your friendship and may result in underlying resentment between you.

Precisely how this conversation should and will play out will obviously vary depending on the circumstances. However, it should follow this general structure:

- ✸ *I'm sorry I* [insert fuck-up here]. e.g. *I'm sorry I haven't been making as much time for our friendship lately.*
- ✸ *I was* [explain what happened]. e.g. *I have been swept up in my new relationship and am struggling to balance it all.*
- ✸ *I really want to make it up to you by* [suggest reparation]. e.g. *I really want to make it up to you. Let's go on a girls' night next weekend to the bar of your choice and the first round is on me.*

The conversation probably won't be as clean as this, but you should make sure you acknowledge what you've done wrong, why it happened and what you're going to do to make it up to your friend. While you can use the apology as an opportunity to give context or an explanation, it's not an opportunity to make excuses or justify your actions.

As well as having a heartfelt conversation, buying or making your friend a thoughtful gift is an effective way of showing you're sorry. It doesn't have to be anything extravagant—just something simple to show that you're sorry and are willing to put in the effort to repair the friendship. Trust us, a bunch of flowers or a bottle of their favourite wine can be a powerful olive branch. You could also shout them dinner, a coffee or a cocktail if you're inviting them out to have the conversation in a public place.

If you're not great at in-person confrontation or easily tongue-tied, you could also apologise by writing your friend a letter.

You could use our earlier guide to an apology as a template to structure your letter. Yes, you could always send them a text, but that doesn't take much effort. There's something more heartfelt and intentional about putting pen to paper and physically writing out an apology. It also gives you an opportunity to explain yourself and how you'll make it up to them without missing any detail that you might not remember when you're feeling stressed in a heated conversation.

If you're super type A like us, you could even type up a draft on your computer and then write it out on paper to make sure you've included everything you need to. Pro tip: spray it with your favourite perfume and seal it with a lipstick kiss for a little extra sparkle.

This is also a great way to apologise to a sensitive friend who may require a more earnest apology than others. They'll appreciate the effort and sincerity, and might even put it in the memory box you know they've got stashed at the top of their wardrobe.

Let go and move on

If you've forgiven your friend and agreed on steps forward in your friendship, it means you can't hold these past mistakes over their head in future. Unless they fall back into their old habits, you need to let it go and start fresh.

You should also only apologise to your friend when you truly mean it—when you're ready to look inward and assess what you've done wrong. As the research and our personal experience shows, saying the words 'I'm sorry' isn't always enough. You need to be open to learning and growing from the situation and demonstrate how you're willing to make it up to the person. If you're unsure you're there yet, you may need to spend a little more time doing the inner work to truly feel remorseful and be ready to apologise.

A note from Sal

My first-ever heartbreak was over my best friend. I'm going to take you back to 2005. The Pussycat Dolls reigned supreme, the air smelled like Dove gradual tanner and the biggest dilemma in my life was whether I was 'Team Ryan' or 'Team Seth'. IYKYK.

I was twelve and the poster child for 'awkward tween' in my first year of high school. Unlike some of my classmates, I was not particularly excited to start Year 7. However, I was lucky enough to transition from my local primary school to a nearby high school, so I'd enter that next chapter of school with a few old friends by my side.

One such friend, let's call her Emma, was my bestie at the time. She lived a couple of streets away. The summer before high school, we spent almost every day surfing, having sleepovers and watching *The Simple Life*.

Although we didn't share any of the same classes, we remained two peas in a pod for the first few terms of Year 7. We both made new friends, but continued to catch the bus together, eat lunch with our group and catch waves on our matching mini mal surfboards most days after school.

That was until the first day of term four. Emma and I had just spent almost two weeks together at my uncle's holiday house on the east coast. As usual, we spent every day with my older sister and her best friend at the beach, surfing, swimming and eating our weight in hot chips. We didn't have any fights or awkward encounters, and when her parents picked her up from my place when we got home, nothing seemed out of the ordinary.

A few days later, on the first day back at school, I walked to the bus stop to find Emma and one of our other BFFs waiting for the bus. I said hi to them both, and while our other friend said 'Hey Sal!' cheerfully, Emma stared at me coldly and then looked away. Our other friend and I looked at each other, confused, and when the bus came, Emma sat next to someone else. Given we'd usually sit next to each other and take one headphone each to listen to something on my Discman, I was shocked to say the least.

That day at school, Emma sat with a different group of girls and continued to ignore me. That night, when I got home from school and hopped on MSN, I asked her what was wrong. She said she didn't want to be my friend anymore and that was that. I was devastated. That night I bawled my eyes out. Dramatically, I ripped up a photo of us that my mum had framed for me. The next day, we both avoided each other at school and it was like we were never friends.

After around six months (which felt like an eternity in high school), I got a notification from her on MSN. She apologised and was asking to be my friend again. While part of me thought I should've been elated, I felt hurt. As silly as it was in the grand scheme of things, I had been betrayed, humiliated and hardened by the experience. While I missed her, the heartbreak and wound to my pride were still very raw. So I refused her olive branch and logged off for the night.

Despite a few well-meaning attempts on her end, I remained stubborn and firm in my stance. But then, slowly but surely, we began to exchange smiles when someone did something stupid on the school bus or we'd pass each other in the playground. By the time we were in Year 10, it felt like a lifetime had passed. We had grown up a lot over that handful of years and I no longer felt the need to hold on to the grudge. I realised I valued the friendship more than my bruised ego.

Emma and I eventually became close again. While we never fully returned to our best friend status, a weight had lifted off my shoulders by forgiving her and mutually agreeing to mend our friendship. And I'm glad we did. While we eventually drifted after high school, I have so many hilarious, wild and fond memories from those few years when we did reconnect. Our time would've ended prematurely if I hadn't moved beyond the heartbreak.

Later, Emma admitted that the reason she hadn't wanted to be my friend anymore was because she wanted to be in the popular group. Starting the new term fresh, if you will. I was hurt but hardly surprised. Even in Year 7, she was (and still is) jaw-droppingly beautiful and charismatic. Meanwhile, I was a late bloomer who needed braces and whose favourite movie was *The Little Mermaid* (spoiler: that last part remains true). Even back then, I was painfully aware that Emma was popular and I was a big dork. But I was happy with the new and old friends I surrounded myself with, and I didn't have any desire to rise up the ranks of the high school social hierarchy.

Over the years we've had conversations about how we both wish that chapter of our friendship hadn't ended that way. At one point she spoke about how different our lives could've been if we remained best friends during those formative years. I didn't really know what to say when she said this. I agreed with her that things would have been different, and despite how hurt little Sally was, we both learned a lot from the experience.

I'll admit, it feels incredibly petty and immature to be a woman in her early thirties recounting this story. I don't hold any resentment towards Emma for what happened. I know she still feels some guilt for the past, but I'm not sure if she should. To be honest, I'd almost forgotten the details of these memories until I revisited them for this book and our podcast.

I gained a lot of perspective reassessing those memories. The friendship itself was never toxic, but how it initially ended certainly wasn't a healthy or nice way to cut ties with a friend who admittedly hadn't done anything wrong. In my angst-ridden youth, I put my pride ahead of the friendship. I later learned that it can be super empowering to forgive someone and let bad energy go. In the right circumstances and with the right boundaries, some friendships are worth reviving. Despite everything, that's a lesson I'm glad I learned early on.

How to know if a friendship is worth saving

Whether you've had a fight with a friend or the relationship has fallen over in a more subtle way, how do you know when a friendship is worth saving? Sometimes it's easier (and wiser) to throw in the towel and call it quits. On the other hand, the commitment and effort required to mend a friendship can bond you in ways that make the relationship stronger. If only you had a crystal ball that could tell you whether the hard work you put into repairing a friendship will pay off. Sadly, this isn't possible, but there *are* a few questions you can ask yourself to determine whether or not a friendship is worth reviving.

First, have you come to a crossroads with this friend before? Most friendships experience some ups and downs over time. However, if you're constantly fighting or regularly questioning a friendship with a particular person, that's a sign that it's probably time to let the friendship go for good. This is especially relevant if the cause of conflict between you two follows a pattern.

Second, is the desire for reconciliation mutual? No matter how pure your intentions are, you can't force your friendship on someone. Regardless of who is in the wrong or what the circumstances are, both parties need to commit to putting in the effort to repair the friendship. Let's say that one friend is in the wrong. That friend obviously needs to do the work to show they're genuinely sorry, have learned from their mistakes and are ready to grow to become a better friend. The *other* friend also needs to make the effort to genuinely accept their friend's apology and move on. There's no point rekindling a friendship if you're not ready to forgive and you're going to hold the person's past wrongdoings over their head.

Another side to this is considering whether the friendship has always been one-sided. Are you always the first to reach out to repair a rift? If so, but you still want to mend the friendship, you should be honest with your friend about how you feel. Sometimes people can inadvertently take their friends for granted, and it's worth giving them the opportunity to step up if you want to set the friendship up for success.

Third, ask yourself *why* you want to continue being their friend. Is it because you share a history with this person? It can be really special to honour the history of a friendship when it's a healthy one. However, the longest friendships aren't always the best ones. If you're only holding on to a friendship because it seems like a waste to let it go after all these years, that's a bad sign. Sometimes friendships run their course and that doesn't discount what they meant to you in the past. However, it is important to recognise when they're no longer serving you or your friend. The real world isn't a high school clique, and you can make the call to cut ties with a long-term frenemy regardless of how long you've known each other if it doesn't make you happy.

That leads us to our fourth question: does this friendship fulfil you and make you happy? Alternatively, does it have the potential to do so if it gets to a healthy place? Sometimes people are just incompatible and that's totally okay. If you're a bit of a people pleaser (Hey! Welcome. You're safe here), it may be a shock to hear that you don't actually have to be friends with or liked by everybody. If the friendship used to be thriving and has since entered its flop era, that's a different story. As we've covered at length, friendships can go through their own seasons. It's totally normal for some to cool off or go through rocky patches at different periods in your life.

On to our fifth question: who are you saving the friendship for? Is it because you have a lot of mutual friends, or because the friend is connected to someone you're dating? At the end of the day, a friendship is supposed to serve both parties in a healthy and fulfilling way. You should be filling up each other's cups. With that in mind, you don't owe anything to anyone else if a friendship is no longer doing that for you. If you're holding on to a friendship out of convenience or obligation rather than from a place of mutual joy, it's probably not worth saving.

Our sixth and final question: what will your life be like if you keep this friendship? This can be a tricky question because no one can predict the future and people do change, but you can use evidence from the past to make an informed decision. Will it be chaotic and drama-filled? Will you feel like you're walking on eggshells or constantly having to compromise? Or will it be full of nights that make you cry with laughter? Moments of you leaning on each other? And incredible memories that'll make the conflict a forgotten moment of the past? If it's the last three, it's worth saving.

When conflict leads to growth

Conflict in a friendship isn't always negative. While it pretty much never feels fun in the moment, conflict can strengthen your friendship. It can bond you and your friend together. It can help you learn more about your friend and yourself. It can help you grow up and become a better friend. It can also help you set healthy boundaries in your friendship that will support it to thrive in the long-term.

Over the last six or so years of our friendship, we've only ever had one major argument. It could've been easily avoided. And we were drunk. Yep, there's a reason why we believe that conflict resolution should happen in an alcohol-free zone. We're living proof that a small dinner and several vodka lime sodas set in a dirty pub in the middle of Sydney is a bad combo.

Working alongside your best friend can be tough. We had been lucky that most of our tiffs prior to this one had been pretty insignificant. That's probably why this argument remains quite fresh in our minds despite a couple of years having passed. While we can agree that we hope it never happens again, we also realise it was an important milestone in our friendship.

In addition to it being a midweek dinner and drinks gone wrong, this was before we took *Two Broke Chicks* solo and it was a high-pressure time for us both. We were having conversations about the future of the brand and our business, which inadvertently also meant the future of our friendship. While neither of us can remember how the argument began or what it was really about, we know that it was a huge vodka-soaked miscommunication. The next morning, we were both cradling heavy hangovers and ended up on the phone crying, apologising and confessing our undying love for one another. As you do.

We both agreed that we couldn't have this exchange completely over the phone, though. While some people would prefer to sweep a drunken row under the rug, we're both super sensitive and knew that wouldn't be the most productive method for our friendship. We knew we had to talk it out face to face. So we sat in Al's car in the underground carpark of Sal's apartment for an hour. We hugged and cried and talked. And hugged some more. And cried some more.

While the spark that fanned the flame of this specific argument wasn't anything serious, the argument itself gave us permission to share how we were feeling with no judgement. It was a chance to air out anything that had been weighing on our shoulders. In that one-hour conversation, we revealed and resolved things that we hadn't even touched on in the conflict the night before. We both acknowledged our own flaws and committed to ways we could improve going forward.

To be honest, all the things we brought up were minor, and if we'd spoken up about them in the moment we could've resolved the tension months or even years before. Even the smallest grievance can grow into a big resentment if you don't communicate it. We brought up things that we might have been tempted to ignore if we didn't share a business together. We're so grateful that we did get the opportunity to have it out and bring these things up—not just for the sake of our business, but for our friendship.

The experience showed us that the healthiest way to deal with conflict in a friendship is to be honest and share how you're feeling when you're feeling it. Otherwise you'll blow up after you've taken advantage of a happy hour deal and find yourself out the front of a bar speaking in tongues.

We probably didn't handle things perfectly, but once we emerged from that car we grabbed an iced latte and some donuts. Within 30 minutes, we were already laughing and crafting comedic tales about how stupid we had been the night before.

We're not saying that every interaction since that day has involved braiding each other's hair and skipping hand in hand while singing 'You're My Best Friend' by Queen. To be honest it hasn't been that far from it, but we've definitely butted heads since then. That's what friends do. But what that argument taught us is that we need to face our problems head-on. We still have work to do and hopefully we'll only get better with time, but we've only become better friends. We've become better communicators. We've become better business partners.

Like an old married couple, we try not to go to sleep mad. If there's tension in the air, we always aim to talk it out within 24 hours. If one of us is in a low mood, we'll communicate to the other to ensure that a big sigh or bitchy remark isn't personal. Sometimes it feels easier to make a passive-aggressive comment and leave the conflict to sort itself out, rather than actually confront it. But then we think back to that morning and how sick we both felt when things weren't right between us. And how easily that feeling of heartbreak (it sounds like we're being dramatic, but that's how it felt) could've been avoided.

We've witnessed other friendships go up in flames in similar scenarios when the alcohol has been flowing and tensions have been running high. The difference we see is that those friends didn't sit down to have the conversation. Neither friend could admit what they had done wrong or what part they had played. Maybe if they'd been upfront and honest, they could be better friends for it. Or maybe their friendship just wasn't meant to be long for this world.

We've learned that conflict doesn't always break a friendship. How you react to it and work to fight *for* the friendship can strengthen it.

If you *really* hate conflict and would prefer to keep the peace rather than potentially stir the pot, we want to leave you with a reminder: resolving an issue with a friend doesn't always have to be a conflict. It can simply be a conversation.

If you approach them from a place of empathy, with belief in your opinion and the goal to improve your friendship, these conversations can actually be really positive experiences for you and your friend. Remember, while it can be tempting, the sole purpose of these interactions isn't to reveal receipts or to prove that your point is the only right one. It's to listen to one another equally and decide *together* how you can move forward.

People match other people's energy. So even if your friend comes in red hot, if you remain calm and confident within yourself then your friend is likely to meet you at your level. With the intention of a genuine resolution, you can both have some of the most honest conversations you can have in a friendship.

TOXIC FRIENDSHIPS

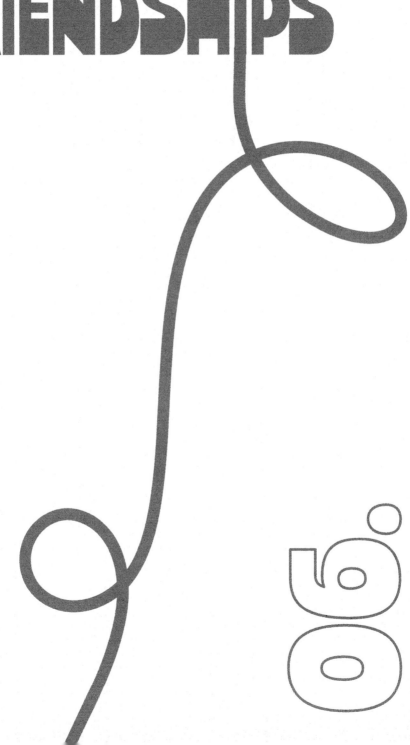

06.

As the ancient proverb (aka internet meme) once said: 'The only toxic we want is "Toxic" by Britney Spears.' This mantra is relevant to workplace dynamics, romantic relationships, family connections and, of course, friendships.

Before we get into toxic friendships we want to break down what 'toxic' actually means. The way 'therapy speak' has been integrated into our vernacular may have done more harm than good to us. People like to throw around weighty terms in irrelevant contexts. Take for example the concept of red and green flags. We might refer to a man wearing sockettes as a red flag. That same guy could believe in equality and we'll call it a green flag instead of the bare minimum. We suggest being mindful how you use these terms so that their true meaning isn't diluted.

In this chapter we're defining toxic friendships as platonic relationships that don't bring you joy or lift you up, that have a toxic effect on your life and your happiness, your true nature and even your ability to be a good friend.

Signs of a toxic friend aren't always super obvious. Sometimes they are clear in the first interaction; sometimes they slowly appear over time. Like any relationship, once-sweet friendships can sour into something completely different as life and people change. You may have lots in common or several mutual friends, yet you leave interactions with them feeling a little more drained than when you arrived.

Toxic friends don't always display Regina George levels of nasty either. They may be the friend who constantly makes sly digs at you but insists they're 'only joking!' Or maybe their smile doesn't *quiiiite* reach their eyes when you tell them you got a pay rise at work. It's the friend who happens to also have a crush on every person you show interest in.

Sometimes it's not so subtle, and you and your friend always end up at each other's throats after a few too many margaritas.

We could go on, but most of us have had at least one run in with a frenemy. Maybe we've even been the toxic friend ourselves. No one can be the most perfect friend every second of every day. It's when these toxic moments become repeated behaviours that it becomes problematic.

A note from Al

I think any self-aware person has experienced a moment when they've felt like a bad friend. I have this battle in my own head from time to time.

Like so many people, I've struggled with my mental health a lot throughout my life. Depression and anxiety kind of feel like toxic friends, always hovering over me waiting to invite themselves in and take over the wheel.

As anyone who struggles in a similar way will know, when this happens it's very hard to like yourself. I have moments when I am so self-critical I'll convince myself of all the reasons I don't like myself and justify why others shouldn't, either.

In these periods when I'm feeling low it's so easy to lock the door and analyse everything I've done wrong. For example, when I was tired and didn't feel like leaving my bed so I bailed on a friend. I couldn't understand why I couldn't get excited for something that I used to look forward to all week. 'What's wrong with me?' says the little voice in my head.

I've experienced moments when exhaustion has gone all the way to my bones, and replying to a friend feels like the hardest task in the world. Which is promptly followed by feelings of guilt because they're being a good friend, reaching out, looking after me, and I can't even take a couple of minutes to respond? 'Wow, I must suck,' says the little voice in my head.

It's when you don't understand yourself that the greasiness of comparison oozes into your thoughts. When you're feeling so sad that you can barely make your bed but then you remember how clean and pristine your friend's room is. 'Why can't you be more like them?' says the little voice in my head.

I could go on and on about all the moments that little voice has told me I'm a bad friend and, in all honesty, some of what it says is true. When we're not our best selves, we're not our best to others. It's a hard pill to swallow and an easy weapon to use against yourself.

However, as my childhood mentor, Hannah Montana, used to say, 'Nobody's perfect.' You cannot always be fucking sunshine and rainbows. You don't have to be.

You can be grumpy and sad and irritable.

You can be lost and insecure and unsure.

Because your friends will understand.

I'm not saying this gives you the right to treat your friends like dirt then turn around and say, 'Oh, sorry, I was having a bad day,' and dust it off like nothing happened.

But I have learned when you're feeling low and worry that you're taking too much from your friends, true friends are there to give you what you need. When you're not strong enough to fight the voices in your head telling you you're not good enough, let your friends fight them for you. Let them in.

I believe that true, healthy friendships are not give-and-take but *give-and-give*. When you need help, you're not taking anything from the people who love you—they're willingly giving it to you.

Always be mindful about how much people can give, though. There are limits and sometimes people abuse these. That's a toxic friendship.

When I think of all the times I've been able to support a friend (and them me), very few instances come to mind where I feel I've been taken advantage of.

More often than not, if you give people the chance to love you, that's exactly what they'll do.

Toxic friend red flags

Toxic friends are no fun. In this section, we're going to reveal some of the common signs to help you identify a toxic friend. If certain friends pop into your head as you read through the list, don't worry. You'll leave the chapter with a bunch of tips on how to deal with and move on from your toxic friend. You may also realise that you're a bit guilty of a few of these behaviours yourself. That's okay, too—it's better to practise awareness and take accountability for these rather than sticking your head in the sand.

You're scared to speak your mind

Most people don't enjoy fighting with their friends, right? If your friend is constantly combative, you may dodge confrontation by agreeing with everything they say. This is a big red flag and could lead to growing resentment the less you feel heard.

A healthy friendship leaves room for disagreements without the need to have a huge blow-up about it. As long as everyone is being respectful, differing opinions can actually help you grow in a friendship.

You may also be afraid to speak up for yourself if you have a friend who always shuts you down. They might always conveniently have an opposing opinion to you, go out of their way to prove you wrong or criticise your opinions for being 'silly' or 'immature'. These disagreements are inevitable in a friendship, but if they're popping up frequently, the signs may point to a toxic friend.

They put you down

Every solid friendship contains some level of gentle roasting when appropriate. For example, it's an unwritten rule that if your friend mispronounces something then you absolutely *have* to give them shit about it for the rest of their lives.

However, there's a difference between a playful dig between mates and constant criticism masked as comedy. Hint: if your friend isn't laughing along with you when you're making the joke, you're probably being a bit of an arsehole.

This type of toxic friend behaviour can also be less obvious. For example, your friend may always magically happen to get the urge to retell the story of that really cringe-worthy time you fell down the stairs as soon as your crush is around.

One of our personal pet peeves is when a friend points out you're turning red during an embarrassing moment. Like, oh really? I couldn't tell that my own head is basically exuding steam as a response to whatever crippling shame job I've just committed.

A note from Sal

Every friendship should be a safe space to poke fun at each other every once in a while. But if you find your feelings are legitimately hurt by your friend's so-called playful jabs, it might be time to speak up for yourself.

I've had a friend make what she thought was a harmless joke at my expense, but it struck a nerve with me. Instead of getting upset and holding it against my friend, I pulled her aside and explained that the joke was making fun of a deep insecurity of mine, and it hurt my feelings. Because she wasn't being intentionally malicious, my friend was so apologetic. She gave me space to say how I felt and never made that same joke again. If she were a toxic friend, she probably would've told me I was overreacting, and that it was 'just a joke'.

They don't celebrate your successes

Your friends should be your biggest hype people. They're the ones who rebrand every loss with a silver lining, and cheer on your successes as if they are their own.

Genuinely sharing in your friends' wins shows a deep level of empathy and compassion. An inability to do so is a sign of jealousy and insecurity. Your friend might rain on your parade and point out flaws when you're sharing the news of a new job opportunity. Or maybe they turn the conversation back on themselves and talk about how much they hate their hair when you return from the salon with amazing new bangs. They might get moody every time you bring up how well things are going with your new love interest.

While it's normal to occasionally feel envious of other people in your life, this shouldn't get in the way of your happiness for them.

They're jealous of your other relationships

Okay, we all make jokes that the ultimate side-eye happens when someone else calls *your* best friend *their* best friend. Like, girl. Are you lost? But, seriously, grown adults can have more than one best friend. If anything, having solid relationships with more than one person is a great sign that should be respected.

A friend may shower you with love and rely a lot on your friendship as their main source of happiness and support— similar to how they would in a romantic relationship. It can be easy to mistake this 'protectiveness' as sweet at first. In reality, though, isolating and guilt-tripping you for investing in other friendships is a form of emotional manipulation.

They're always the main character

Everyone is the main character of their own story. However, some friends don't just think they're the star of their own life—they believe they're playing the leading role, supporting cast, writer and producer of *your* story, too. In other words, they're a bit narcissistic. These friends have a knack for making themselves the centre of every situation. It's not until they've spilled every detail of their life and you're about to pay the bill that they hastily ask, 'So how've you been?'

If drama seems to follow your friend wherever they go, this is another red flag. No one's life is smooth sailing 100 per cent of the time—but if your mate is constantly fighting with friends or in the middle of a crisis at work, the common denominator may be them. Instead of drama following them, the reality is that they might actually be chasing it.

While there will be times when one person in a relationship may need to demand a little more attention, friendships should be balanced overall. You shouldn't feel like the sidekick in your friend's one-person show.

It feels like a competition

A little healthy competition might be fine in your work or school life, but it has no place in friendships. Some friends always have to one-up you. They're always more tired than you, more overworked than you and more hard done by than you. Rather than hyping you up when you look super hot before a night out, you'll notice they become a little icy or passive aggressive.

While it's only natural to feel jealous or envious of our friends sometimes, the difference between a toxic friend and a good friend is how they choose to act on these feelings.

They're always gossiping

If we claimed not to love a little gossip between good friends, we'd be straight-up liars. However, ranting or bitching about someone shouldn't make up the majority of your conversations with your friends. If you're in your twenties and beyond and you find yourself with a friend who still bitches about people they went to high school with, it's probably time to suggest some new talking points.

According to a study published in *Social Psychological and Personality Science*, gossiping is a social skill that helps humans stay connected and progress. However, a friendship based on nothing but bitching about other people only spreads negativity and gross vibes. Plus, when a friend is constantly complaining about people in their lives, you can't help but question how they must speak about you to others.

They don't help out

Sometimes it's the small things that point out the toxicity of a friendship. When a friend doesn't help you out, big or small, this could be a sign of weaponised incompetence or straight up being inconsiderate. If you're not familiar with the term weaponised incompetence, it refers to a behaviour pattern where someone pretends to be bad at something to get out of shared responsibilities. This may be why friendships sometimes feel one-sided. Your friend may know that you'll pick up the slack, so they don't even bother putting in the effort or make excuses to get out of it.

Some examples:

- ⊛ They don't help clean up the dishes when you get takeaway or make dinner because they 'suck at cleaning'.
- ⊛ They don't help with any planning when you're booking a holiday together because 'you're the "type A friend" and way more organised'.
- ⊛ They don't offer a hand when you've got a big task on your plate, such as moving house or picking up a killer Facebook Marketplace find.
- ⊛ They don't return the items you've loaned them unless you pick them up yourself.

The friendship feels one-sided

It's pretty common for one person to take the reins more than the other at times in any relationship dynamic. However, if you're constantly the one to organise catch-ups or send 'How was your weekend?' texts, it can be suuuper frustrating.

We've both made the hard decision to stop reaching out to a friend to see if they'd make contact. We both found that neither of our friends contacted us. While this is shitty, at least you know—and it can be a good opportunity to either let the friendship peter out or bring up how you're feeling directly with your mate.

Life lessons from our chicks
Real-life wisdom fresh from our DMs

Don't give your love and time to those who don't have either for you.

They don't take accountability

No friend is perfect. But mature friends know how to own up to their mistakes, admit when they're wrong and apologise. If your friend is constantly sweeping things under the rug or gaslighting you into thinking that they haven't done anything wrong, this is a toxic friend.

A note from Al

I've always had the mentality that nothing bad can come from saying sorry and nothing good can come from digging your heels in, doubling down and stubbornly committing to the idea you did nothing wrong.

If someone's feelings are hurt, it takes no skin off your back to say sorry for your part.

There have been moments in which I've unintentionally upset a friend, as I'm sure a lot of readers will relate to. I always try not to get defensive or tell my friend they've taken things too personally or the wrong way. Their feelings are hurt and I *am* sorry for that.

If a friend can't empathise when you're upset with something that's happened, even if it wasn't on purpose, that's not a friend with your best interests at heart.

There are obviously boundaries that come with this—for instance, if a friend claims you said something you didn't, saying you're sorry may not be the healthiest way forward.

You leave feeling drained

You should look forward to seeing your friends and leave them feeling happier than when you arrived. If an interaction with a friend completely drains your social battery and leaves you feeling low, insecure or anxious, you may have a toxic friend on your hands. This may be a result of them constantly complaining, dumping their drama on you or passive aggressiveness that leaves you feeling on edge during the entire interaction.

If you find that you're looking for excuses to bail on this friend or you get a tight feeling in your chest leading up to hanging out with them, listen to your gut instinct. Your body is literally telling you that this friendship isn't serving you. In a study published in the *Psychology and Aging* journal conducted over 30 years, researchers found that low-quality friendships in your twenties and thirties have a significant long-term impact on your emotional wellbeing later in life. This is because it's the relationships we make in these formative years that shape our opinions, values, self-worth and how we deal with interpersonal relationships in life.

A note from Al

I had a good friend, Madison, who'd been through a hell of a year: the whole works of a shitty situationship, work stress, money troubles and more. Obviously, as her friend, I was more than happy to be there for her through it all.

However, fast forward three years and being 'hard done by' had unfortunately become one of her personality traits. Whenever we hung out the entire conversation would be about whatever negative thing happened to her that week or what she was stressed about. Madison stopped checking in with me and it kind of felt like our hang-outs were one-sided therapy sessions. I'd leave our conversations feeling super tired, sad and, you guessed it, drained af.

It upset me because I'd really loved our friendship beforehand. I also felt guilty because whenever Madison would ask to hang out I'd feel stressed about how draining the conversation would be. I'd beat myself up because I knew she'd had a tough time a few years ago. I felt like I was a bad friend for not always wanting to be a punching bag for complaints and negativity.

After multiple attempts to try to open up the friendship to more positive waters, I made the decision to protect my space and distance myself slightly until I felt mentally prepared to support her again. The friendship always left my cup empty. Once my cup had refilled enough to have a bit of overflow I re-engaged with her, but started implementing boundaries around our friendship such as spending time in group settings so that it was harder for her to dump on me.

They get mad at you for being busy

Life gets busy and it's as simple as that. Maybe you have a lot on at work or you're just having a bit of a down day/week/month. You don't need the added stress of your friends getting on your back for not replying to texts, already having plans or simply needing time to yourself. A friend guilt-tripping you for forgetting to reply to a text or not being able to make it to Friday drinks can be a warning sign that they expect you to drop everything for them rather than respecting your own boundaries and needs.

A note from Al

So I can be a bit notorious for going off the grid here and there. Whether it's a day, week or sometimes a month, I'll go into my cave (aka not leaving my apartment) to re-centre myself. Sometimes this happens after a really big social month of birthdays and travelling, or when I just need a beat to enjoy some of my alone activities.

For a really long time I would apologise and feel bad for needing this time to recharge. I thought I needed to be available for my friends at all times. Whenever I realised I missed a message or didn't want to go somewhere, my response always started with 'I'm so sorry' followed by some long-winded excuse.

But why was I apologising?

Should I have to apologise because I'm taking care of myself? No.

Wouldn't friends want me to look after my mental health so when I do spend time with them I'm at my best? Obviously.

This realisation made the cogs click into place for me. It illuminated the red and green flags in my friendships. It empowered me to be honest with my friends. Instead of giving them a long-winded excuse as to why I wasn't coming out that weekend or hadn't replied to their text, I was honest that I needed to hibernate for a bit.

True friends have always respected my boundaries. Very few people in my life have responded to me with some sort of passive-aggressive response.

I think we forget that we all need a little time to regroup and regather, and friends who want the best for us will always support that.

Next time you're overwhelmed by your social calendar or life—because it will very likely happen—try being honest with your friends. I'm sure you'll be pleasantly surprised by the majority response. Worst-case scenario is that you filter out the weeds.

They exclude you

You can't expect to be invited to everything. Even in a group dynamic, it's totally normal for friends to seek out one-on-one time with each other. However, if your friends are frequently leaving you off the guest list or texting in a group chat that you're not involved in, that's a horrible feeling. Perhaps you notice they don't include you in conversations in group situations or only communicate through personal jokes that you're not involved in when you're around. Sometimes this is an honest mistake, but it can also be a very intentional and pointed intimidation tactic.

Life lessons from our chicks
Real-life wisdom fresh from our DMs

Wait for your people, they are out there! It's okay not to get along with everyone.

They only hang out with you when they need you

We have to admit, there's nothing better than a friend with skills: the friend who owns a cake-making business and whips up the most Pinterest-worthy treats for your birthday, or the friend who is a make-up artist and acts as your very own glam squad before a night out. Of course it's fine to ask your talented friends for an occasional favour or take advantage of their mates rates. However, if you're only asking your friend to hang out when you want to use them for something, that's a big ick.

A note from Sal

My friend B used to be a hairstylist but has since switched career paths into a completely different industry. However, she still does some hairdressing from home to make some extra cash when she has spare time. She's known for being very generous with her rates, and some people definitely take that for granted.

While B was more than happy to do her friends' hair, she noticed that a handful of people would only reach out to her when they wanted a cheap haircut. When she'd ask them if they wanted to hang out away from her at-home salon basin, they'd conveniently be busy—but ensured they could catch up the next time they needed a bleach and tone. These friends would also be quite cold to B if she turned down an appointment because she had other commitments scheduled or was simply too exhausted after work.

While I suggested B should shave a dirty word in the back of their head for revenge during their next appointment, she took the more mature route and told her friends how she felt. Most of them completely understood, apologised for their behaviour and made more of an effort to book in quality time to hang out beyond their bi-monthly hair appointment.

Toxic friendship groups

It's common to find that an individual friend is a bit of a bad apple—but what if you come across an entire batch that's gone rotten?

Yep, you can have an entire friendship group that oozes toxicity.

Toxic conversation, values, behaviour and habits can feed from person to person, and due to the environment it just catches. Humans can very much have a pack mentality and the fear of being left out or rejected can influence our behaviours. Basically, what we're saying is: peer pressure can make you a bit of an arsehole.

A toxic friendship group is where friends belittle one another, gossip about each other and mask it as 'venting', pressure each other into doing things they don't want to do and always make each other feel like they're in a constant state of fight or flight.

If everyone in your friendship group is always complaining, ostracising outsiders and enforcing like-mindedness they may be succumbing to groupthink. According to psychologist Irving Janis, groupthink is where a group of well-intentioned and well-mannered friends make immoral, subjective or irrational decisions that are driven by a hive mentality. It's when a group has only two options: conform or conflict. These moments can be as small as deciding where to go for someone's birthday dinner or whether someone is 'allowed' to invite a friend from work they just met. It's okay for wolves and dolphins to have a pack mentality and be run by groupthink. Not your friends.

Here are some signs your group is toxic and it's time to take a step back:

- there is a 'leader'
- you feel like you're always walking on eggshells
- everyone talks about 'we' and 'the group' rather than acknowledging individual wants and needs
- everyone gives outsiders the cold shoulder
- you don't feel like you can share your opinion if it's different to the group.

If this sounds a bit too familiar, it's time to branch out and make some new connections in your life. While one toxic friendship may be salvageable, an entire group of toxic friends is a beast that is not your job to conquer.

It can be really difficult to come to terms with the fact your entire friendship group is toxic. It's a hard pill to swallow, a moment of realisation and self-awareness that might put you into panic mode. But remember: unlike in the animal kingdom where there is safety in numbers, you do not need to spend your time with a group that promotes toxicity. These friends are not your key to survival. You don't 'need' them.

We're not saying you must have a huge monologue moment and tell everyone why you're 'leaving the group'. A slow fade-out is as effective as a simple goodbye.

Yes, they may (and probably will) have some things to say about you behind your back, but if they're toxic, they were very likely already doing that so it's a bit of a *meh* thought.

We know this is no simple task, though, and it can be incredibly scary.

A note from Al

In hindsight, my young adulthood friendship group was kind of 'all of the above' in the red flag department.

It's very important to start with the fact that not every memory I have of these friends is bad, and not one person from the group is completely evil in my eyes. I don't hate them in the slightest or wish them ill will. But when I think about my time in this friendship group, I'm glad it's behind me.

A lot of what you've read so far in this section applied to my situation. There was a group leader who was serving Harriet, head girl from the movie *Wild Child* (IYKYK), constant bitching about people, referring to ourselves as a group rather than the individuals we were, and so on.

'The group wants to go to El Cantina.'

'The group thinks we should do New Year's at Sarah's instead.'

'The group doesn't really know her so we're going to keep movie night as just us.'

I got wrapped up in the sense of belonging to a group that for so long I didn't realise how toxic it had become. After struggling through friendships in high school I was so scared of being on the out and alone. I was so happy to finally be included that I overlooked the red flags.

Maybe 'overlooked' isn't the right term; rather, 'consciously ignored'.

I noticed when someone would roll their eyes when I spoke. I noticed when they all posted pictures of themselves on Instagram Stories hanging out, but the plans weren't in the group chat that I was in. I noticed when they would laugh at others' jokes but not mine. I noticed when I said I agreed with something, even though I didn't. I noticed when they cut a girl out of the group for no reason at all, and I said nothing because I was scared to be next.

I eventually realised that I didn't truly belong with these people, and it was one of the reasons I moved away from my hometown. I still kept in touch with everyone, but I slowly distanced myself more and more while expanding my connections elsewhere.

However, one night when I went back to visit and grab some drinks with everyone, a vibe misread occurred leading to a rumour being spread about me and my relationship. As you can imagine, my group of so-called friends took the opportunity to tear me apart over it. I had proof the rumour wasn't true, but it didn't matter.

Their essay-length texts and complete shunning broke me. Even though this isn't the behaviour of true friends, I panicked at the thought of being alone. Their words were slung and found their mark.

After some time, a few girls in the group reached out to say they were sorry—but only after they discussed in a group chat whether they would do so. To my knowledge, not one decided they would do so off their own bat.

In hindsight, this fallout was one of the best things to happen to me. As I mentioned at the start, there is no animosity between us now and I wish everyone the best. It gave me the freedom to open myself up, work on myself and gain the security of being my own best friend—which, in turn, allowed me to find my real people later in life.

If you're stuck in a toxic friendship group, I just want to give you a hug. It really sucks. It's scary and lonely and you often don't even know how you ended up there.

What I want you to know is that nothing bad can come from you unshackling yourself from negativity. You can allow yourself to find and foster new friendships. I look at my friends now and the love I feel for them and they for me, and I want to go back and tell my past self: 'Don't worry. Your people are coming and, I promise you, they will laugh at your jokes.'

How to cut ties with a toxic friend

Toxic friendships aren't always black and white. Sometimes a friend is going through a rough patch and it's worth waiting out (and supporting them through) the storm. Sometimes you just need to press pause on the friendship, go your separate ways and come back together when you're both ready. Other times, you've grown into different people—or maybe you were always incompatible—in which case you might be better off cutting ties altogether. But how do you know which fork in the road to take, and how to do it?

To paraphrase Albus Dumbledore: it takes a lot of bravery to stand up to our enemies, but it takes even more to stand up to our friends.

But without a conversation, tensions typically only compound over time and your annoyance with your friend can quickly turn into a very poisonous resentment. If you think a friendship is worth saving, it's absolutely worth bringing up the issue sooner rather than later. We covered *exactly* how to handle this conflict in Chapter 5.

But let's say that conversation didn't go as planned or your friend continues to be a bit shit, or they've done something so unforgivable you don't even want to save the friendship. It's time to cut ties. It sounds intense, but it doesn't have to be dramatic or a result of a big blowout fight.

Like any break-up there's no one-size-fits-all formula to ending a friendship, but here are two strategies you could consider.

The fade-out

Sometimes a friendship can fizzle out on its own. If you feel like you're the only one putting any effort into your friendship, you can take a step back and see what happens. If your hypothesis was correct and the friendship is indeed one-sided, it's very likely that you won't hear from your friend and the friendship will naturally fade.

This kind of fade-out is very different to ghosting, though. We're not saying you should stop replying to your friends or disappear from their life without a word. Unless they're being abusive and really toxic, ghosting is a bit of a brutal way out. If your friend *does* reach out and you still want to end the relationship, it may be time for the tough conversation.

The tough conversation

The tough conversation is likely to be emotional, but it doesn't have to be a screaming match or lengthy debate. To make sure you stay on track, you might want to make a mental note of your key talking points beforehand. Explain why the friendship is no longer serving either of you and that it would be better for you both to end the relationship now. Then there's no need for the obligatory 'let's catch up' text when you don't want to. If you end things cordially, this also means that you can still be in the same room without any awkwardness if you have mutual friends.

Again, this is a conversation that should be had either in person or over the phone. It's pretty poor form to end a friendship via text—especially if you've been friends for a long time. There are some things that can't be summarised in a few sentences and some emojis, ya know?

Supporting yourself through a friendship break-up

At the end of the day, a friendship break-up is hard. Sometimes it can be even harder than a romantic break-up. We know from experience.

When we enter romantic relationships we don't go on a first date thinking we've met our forever person. Cheque, please! We go in with the underlying expectation that things may not work out in the long run. But we expect friendships to be around forever—because why wouldn't they? When we do lose a friend, it can be a shock. We not only feel the loss of past experiences but the future moments we thought we'd share together.

Friendship break-ups, in our opinion, are completely underrated in terms of how deeply they can wound you. The heartache can leave you feeling betrayed, embarrassed and bitter. And it's more common than you think.

If you have decided to leave a friendship in the past, there are a few things to remember.

First, be proud of yourself. It's not easy to put yourself first and so many of us struggle with this. We're told to put others' feelings before our own, so when we prioritise ourselves it can feel wrong and sometimes even selfish. In this moment, take a second to feel pride for being your own best friend right now.

Be kind to yourself. When you lose any relationship there is going to be a time of mourning. Whether you knew this person for a month or your whole life, it's going to be a process to let go and be okay with what happened. During this time be understanding and gentle with yourself, because it's not easy going through a friendship break-up.

Be honest with yourself. One thing us humans are fabulous at doing is second-guessing ourselves. You may find yourself wondering, 'Was it really that bad?' or 'Was I being dramatic?' In these moments you have to remain honest with yourself about why you made the decisions you did and trust your gut, because nine times out of ten it knows what's best for you.

In these times of friendship heartache there is a saying that can be a source of comfort: 'If you're not losing friends, you're not growing up.' While this obviously doesn't mean you need to dump every person you know to be an adult, it does show that change is a part of life. As we grow our needs, values and wants evolve with our experiences. Sometimes the people in our lives are able to grow alongside us; other times they're not.

It can be incredibly heart-wrenching to say goodbye to a person who felt like home. But when it's time, you do have to let them go. If you hold on too tightly and fight it, you're filling up space inside your soul that is meant for your future people. You're wasting your love, energy and friendship on people who can no longer receive it rather than those who deserve it. (And you may not even know those people yet.)

If you're holding on to something that's weighing you down, you're not allowing yourself to be free to find new people. Things end for no reason or big reasons but there is still an end. Find closure in the fact that you have to close chapters to finish your own book of life.

We give you the green light to choose your friends wisely. Know your own value and the worth of your friendship. Nourishing and prioritising healthy friendships can only lead to living a fulfilled life.

Dear Sal and Al

How can I recover and move forward after a good friend has done me wrong? Help!

Hey chick,

Firstly, we're so sorry you're going through this. Friendship break-ups can honestly feel just as bad (if not worse) than romantic break-ups.

Give yourself permission to mourn this loss in your life. Ugly cry, vent to your loved ones and stomp around the house feeling sorry for yourself. What you're feeling is completely valid. You're not being dramatic. You have potentially lost a really important person in your life and that heartbreak is real. If you don't allow yourself to feel the emotions in the moment, they have a way of building up in the background of your brain and exploding at a later date.

Once you've had a chance to cry it out, it's time for you to invest in some serious 'me time'. Take yourself on some solo dates and start romanticising time with yourself. Whether it's a cheesy rom-com flick with a popcorn combo, a mani-pedi or long beach swim, prioritise doing things that make you happy. Basically, you want to be your own best friend. (Flip back to Chapter 1 if you need a reminder on exactly how to do this!)

As well as prioritising your relationship with yourself, you should also lean on your other friends and loved ones for support right now. Even if you've lost a really good friend in your life, you're not alone. As well as sharing how you're feeling, making new memories with other people will help you get through this. Message an old friend to catch up for coffee or ask a workmate if they want to head to a nearby happy hour this Friday. Start putting yourself out there! Return to Chapter 4 if you need some handy hints to broaden your social circle.

If you feel like this loss is really weighing on you and seeping into other parts of your life, try reaching out for some professional help. It could be really helpful to get an unbiased perspective and expert tips on how to manage your emotions during this tough time.

If this friend really hurt you, boundaries will also help you get through this. It might feel a little brutal, but muting or blocking them on social media can help protect your peace. The pang of scrolling through your feed and coming across a photo of them and their new bestie probably isn't going to be very helpful.

Remember that just because one friend has done you dirty, not all of your friendships are doomed to have the same fate. Most of your friends will have your best interests at heart and would never intentionally hurt you. So try not to carry this mistrust into your other friendships, because it could stop you from making the deep connections that'll help you move on.

Your old friend's behaviour isn't a reflection of you or your worth. You deserve to be loved and to have sincere friendships. This friendship break-up will help you learn what you do and don't want from your relationships from now on. This is just the start of another amazing chapter for you.

Good luck!

Lots of love,

Sal and Al

FRIENDSHIPS VERSUS ROMANTIC RELATION- SHIPS

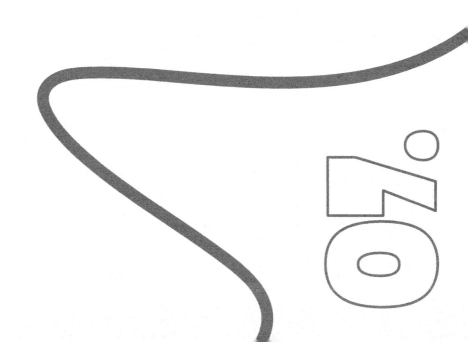

07.

It's easy to assume there's an immediate conflict between friendships and romantic relationships. There can be a tug of war of importance. Friends and partners have such different, complex and deep roles in our lives it's often hard to juggle both—but, importantly, it's not impossible.

From experience, we've learned how to balance romantic relationships and friendships and we're here to share what we've learned—a lot of which came from making mistakes. It's easy to do. Maybe you've ditched a friend to see your crush, or lied about meeting up with your shitty ex because you didn't want your friend to get mad at you. Maybe you've become a bit too wrapped up in a relationship and, once that ended, looked around and found that your friends hadn't waited for you.

The experience of friendship is vastly different when you're single versus when you're in a relationship. There's an essence of independence when you're single. You don't have to consider anyone else's calendar besides your own, and you don't have to play the game of juggling friendships and partners. The list goes on.

No matter what your current relationship status, this chapter will help you deal with conflict between friends and partners, feeling like you've lost a friend to their relationship, that isolating experience when you're the last single friend left and beyond.

How to handle being the only single friend

There is nothing wrong with being single! Everyone is on their own trajectory. We're all allowed to weigh up our own values. Travelling, building your career and spending time on your own are just as significant as finding a romantic life partner.

We're fed a narrative that if you're not in a relationship, there's something undesirable about you. This is especially the case for women: if you're single you might fear you'll be perceived as some kind of spinster. (Side note: we recently learned that in ye olden times, a single woman over 25 was called a thornback. No joke. We think it's the coolest title and have contemplated changing our last names.) Obviously this is a completely out-of-date notion. There are many reasons why you may be single: whether you're fresh out of a relationship, in your independent era or there are only dud fish in the sea.

That said, being the only single person you know can be challenging and frustrating. It can feel isolating at times, too. You might feel excluded, and it can be incredibly exhausting constantly being asked, 'So are you seeing anyone at the moment?' (Why do we always have to be dating someone? Stop asking this of your single friends!)

We promise, being single is not the end of the world. There isn't anything wrong with you, and it's better to be right on your own than wrong with someone else. That all being said, it can be easy to start comparing your own timeline to others, so here are some ways to embrace the beautiful independence that is your single era.

Avoid the comparison game

Stop comparing your own love life to the loved-up relationships on social media. It's not a factual representation. In fact, a study published by *Psychology Today* showed that when people make 'excessive' posts about their significant others, it's often a sign of an unhappy relationship. Of course that's not to say every couple that posts loved-up photos on Facebook is unhappy, but comparing ourselves only pulls our focus from what we actually want towards what others have that we don't. Half the time we don't even want what others have; we just think we do! Comparison can also cause resentment to build within your friendships. Our advice is to throw this mindset straight out the window.

Take yourself on dates

Spending time alone is one of the most beautiful parts of being single. You can do whatever you want to do whenever you want to do it.

Don't spend all your time in your pyjamas reading smut books (definitely still do this, but within moderation). Make sure you're taking yourself out on single dates, such as going to the movies on your own, heading to the beach with a good podcast or seeing the latest exhibition at a museum. Spend time dating yourself—it's one of the best things you'll get to do for yourself.

If you're not comfortable doing these things on your own yet, start by asking a friend to join you, and slowly start spending time on your own too.

Set boundaries with your friends

Your friends shouldn't be a package deal with their partners. If you want to see your mates and *just* your mates without their significant other trotting along, tell them that.

A lot of the time people don't realise they're doing this. Asking them for some one-on-one time will probably be easier than you think.

In saying that, there will be times to embrace the third, fifth or seventh-wheel vibes. We can't expect friends to *never* bring their partners to social outings, but we can expect there to be a balance.

Al was Sal's third wheel/adopted child for years. She'd come over for sleepovers and hang out with Sal and her partner Chris and they all loved every second of it.

Your wants can look different to others'

A successful life is not measured by the cheesy rom-com fairytale standard of falling in love, getting married and having a family. There's nothing wrong with you for not wanting things your friends do, and vice versa.

To paraphrase Meg March from *Little Women*, just because your dreams are different from your friends', it doesn't mean they're unimportant.

Embrace this era

A romantic relationship is not a measure of success—for some it's not a goal in life at all. A 2014 study showed that those in relationships and those who are single have similar ratings of overall wellbeing. A relationship does not necessarily equal joy, happiness or fulfilment.

Being single does not have to be a chore. Going on bad dates and giggling to your friends about the tiny thing that gave you 'the ick' is *fun*. Embrace the chaos that is being single. Lean in to the ability to create your own path, make your own decisions and spend time with your mates—whether they're single or not!

A note from Al

When my ex dumped me, I thought the world was ending, hell was freezing over and I'd never feel joy again. (It sounds a bit dramatic, but so am I, to be fair.) But after doing some self-reflection and working on myself, I started to understand the power of being single.

I'd been in relationships between the ages of 18 and 23. Those years are so important to forming the foundations of who we are as adults. That's not to say you can't find yourself if you're in a relationship, but in the ones I had, there was no room for self-growth. Looking back, I definitely forgot who I was.

I only met my true self when I was single in my early to mid-twenties. Through trial and error, I discovered and rediscovered the things I loved doing on my own, with friends and on dates. My years as a single girl will forever hold a special place in my heart. I had one person to answer to: myself.

However, if I could describe this period of my life in one way it would be 'girlhood'. The friendship between a single gal and her single girlfriends is unmatched. It's unhinged, in the best way possible. It's late-night phone calls and giggling about the terrible first date you just had. It's being in your daggy trackpants then minutes later being ready to go out on the town because your friend texts you that they're bored. It's silently agreeing not to discuss the person you kissed the night before.

Being single with single friends is a combination of exhilarating, chaotic and pure. You're kind of like each other's romantic partner in the way that you hang out, cuddle and look after each other.

It's a big part of why I never felt the need to rush into a relationship. I truly didn't feel like anything was missing. I knew that when I started dating someone, I would have less time to spend with my friends simply because there's only 24 hours in a day and seven days in a week.

I would often say I hated first dates because they had a 50/50 chance of going well or being a horrible waste of my time, whereas hanging out with my friends was a 100 per cent guaranteed good time.

When I met my now partner I did feel like I was abandoning my single friends in a way. I didn't want them to feel like we could no longer relate to each other's lives, or that I'd become that friend who, in a condescending tone, says 'It will happen when you least expect it!'

At the end of the day, there is nothing wrong with living it up as a single person or loving it up in a relationship. Neither takes away from your value. Your relationship status will never determine your ability to be a good friend.

Navigating friendships when you're in a relationship

While many people mistake us for a romantic couple, we're actually both very loved-up in relationships and therefore experts on this topic. If you've read this far, you know we believe that no one person can completely fill your cup. As well as a solid relationship with yourself, you need lots of different dynamics with others in your life to feel fulfilled. No matter how great your other half is, them alone will not be enough. We hate to break it to ya.

We weren't born masters of juggling friendships and romantic dynamics. There has been a lot of trial and error as we've navigated romances and friendships over the years. Within our friendship alone, we've represented the two opposite ends of the spectrum. Sal has been dating her partner for over 16 years at the time of writing. Al is also in a stable, happy relationship, but has experienced the highs and lows of heartbreak, dating and falling in love over the last couple of years.

While we truly believe it's very possible to maintain friendships alongside romantic relationships, it can be bloody hard at times. Between holding down a career, drinking eight glasses of water a day, getting 10,000 steps in, doom-scrolling on TikTok plus making time for yourself, your friends and your lover, it's no surprise the chicks out there are struggling.

A note from Sal

I believe the key to successfully balancing friends and romance is making a conscious effort to prioritise both.

For the first eight years of dating my partner Chris, we were in a semi-long-distance relationship. Given I was still in high school and at uni for a big chunk of this time, I could only see Chris on the weekends. I learned very quickly that you don't need to be glued to your partner's hip to have a flourishing relationship. I mean, they do say distance makes the heart grow fonder, right? I would spend quality time with Chris on the weekends and use weeknights to study, catch up with friends and binge *The Hills*.

I also learned to communicate directly with friends and Chris about when I needed to spend quality time with other people. If it was my best friend's birthday party on a Saturday, sorry, babe. We can't hang out this weekend. That's because these relationships exist in harmony, not in a hierarchy. They all need their own levels of attention, and sometimes the attention levels will ebb and flow. While this meant Chris and I sometimes went weeks without seeing each other, we both understood how important it is to make space and foster friendships with other people.

Both of us now live with our respective partners. Funnily enough, we've both been warned that living with your partner can put pressure on the relationship or isolate you from your friends. While we know this to be true in many cases, neither of us were particularly worried about that. We make a conscious effort to spend time with our friends sans partners regularly. While double dates or group hangs with a mix of both single and coupled-up friends can be fun, you need to spend solo time with your friends, too.

Next time you're thinking of inviting your partner to dinner with your mates, pause and ask yourself if you really need them there with you. Your mates may say it's fine, but you can't bitch about your partner leaving their wet towel on the bathroom floor if they're there. The top-tier shit-talking that makes up the best of friendships just isn't possible with people's partners around.

It's also important to make memories that are exclusive to you and your friends. So many of our favourite memories are ones we've shared with our platonic pals. They're the types of memories that still make us almost pee with laughter just by thinking about them. The bonding moments that happen during D&Ms on hot girl walks can act as the foundations of friendship. It may sound silly, but these moments with your friends are life-shaping and fucking important.

It's also key to leave your partner at home physically *and* mentally. Your friends probably don't care about how funny it was when your partner accidentally wore their underwear back to front to work. Obviously your friends love that you're in love, but they don't always need to be hearing about every single cute thing you two did that week.

Plus, spending time apart gives you something to talk about with your partner. If each of your experiences are almost identical because you spend every second together, it leaves almost nothing to talk about. It's important to grow both as a couple and also as individuals.

If you feel like you're not prioritising your friendships and a few alarm bells are ringing in your head right now, don't stress. These habits can be unlearned and improved upon.

Reconnecting with friends after prioritising your romance

If you haven't made an effort with your friends recently, don't be surprised if they're a little hurt or pissed. It may be awkward at first, but just rip it off like a bandaid. Call up your friend or shout them brekkie and let it all out. Feel free to paraphrase, but the conversation can start off a little something like this:

> *I'm so sorry I haven't been very present or prioritising our friendship recently. I really miss you and value our friendship, so I'm going to make more of an effort to balance all of my relationships from now on.*

If your friend doesn't bring it up, it might be tempting to sweep it under the rug and try to repair the friendship without the awkward apology. Trust us, though: it's worth initiating the conversation. Your friend will appreciate you acknowledging their feelings and this will make them more likely to be willing to reconnect.

If your friend has been trying to reach out and you haven't reciprocated, the ball is now in your court. Invite them over for dinner or a sleepover, see a movie together or suggest an ongoing activity that you can do together, such as a Pilates class or weekly walks.

A note from Sal

I've seen many friends prioritise their romantic relationship over friendship, only for their love affair to come crashing down. For a long time, my instinct when it happened was to roll my eyes or say 'I told you so.' Perhaps it's because almost every couple in my extended family, including my own parents, has experienced divorce. The same goes for my friends and acquaintances: sadly, many of the weddings I've attended in the last ten years have already ended in separation. (I'm starting to think I might be a bad luck charm and need to sage myself before accepting a wedding invitation.) I've seen firsthand how even the most solid-seeming relationships can fold over time, and how important it is to have a separate support system when you need it.

I also think that focusing your life solely on another person is an incredibly limiting way to live. It's only natural to form similar interests, opinions and hobbies with your partner. That's called being compatible. Hell, when I look back on old photos I've noticed that mine and Chris's hairstyles have been literal mirror images as we've grown up together. However, there's a difference between having mutual interests with your partner and throwing away your life to fit in with theirs.

I've seen friends removing piercings, changing hairstyles and adopting completely different fashion styles at their partner's request. I've seen friends give up hobbies or tone down personal interests they loved because their partner thought they were silly. I know friends whose social circles slowly have became entirely made up of their partner's friends.

The most common and heartbreaking thing I've seen, though, is friends losing their sparkle and what made them so special. I'd realise my friend laughed less when we caught up. The things that used to light them up with passion had been put on the backburner. Their big smile didn't quite reach their eyes like it used to. Then, if they left these all-consuming relationships, I was happy to notice their sparkle return.

That is why I think it's so important to continue spending time with your friends regardless of your relationship status. Your mates will encourage you to talk in silly voices and snort with laughter. They'll remind you of things that bring you joy and make you special. Your friends can be the anchor that'll keep you true to who you really are.

When your friend ditches you for their significant other

This is gonna strike a nerve with some of y'all, we know. We all have a friend (or perhaps have been the friend) who completely throws themselves into the deep end whenever they enter a relationship. As they focus all of their energy on spinning the plates of their romance, their other plates occupied by family and friends become neglected and come crashing to the floor. One unanswered text message and bailed-on plan at a time, the friendship grows distant and eventually flatlines. That's until cracks start to form in their relationship. They sheepishly return from the Bermuda Triangle that was their dating life to seek your sage advice, a shoulder to cry on or a girl's night out.

We've both been the discarded friend in this situation and it fucking sucks. You feel taken for granted, unappreciated and tossed aside. So when your friend does come crawling back, it can be tempting to roll your eyes. While justified, this probably isn't the kindest or most mature action plan.

It's also good to do some self-reflection here. Is your friend *really* spending all of their time with their significant other, or arc you just used to them spending all of their time with you?

It's only natural for our investment in particular friendships to change over time. Mathematically speaking, we only have 24 hours in every day so our time with friends will automatically diminish when we enter a relationship. It's also pretty natural for most of us to invest more of our time, emotions and energy into romantic connections than platonic ones. Of course, this isn't an excuse to completely ditch your friends when someone enters your life. However, we're the first to admit that we've experienced irrational jealousy or annoyance when our ride-or-die starts spending more time with their partner. Like, what do you mean I'm not the only person in your life?

Life lessons from our chicks

Real-life wisdom fresh from our DMs

I was so naive when I met my first boyfriend, allowed myself to be consumed by the relationship and had to reconnect with a lot of old friends I had lost once we broke up.
I promised in my next relationship I would remember that, and ensure that my future partner and I would make time to do things on our own with our friends.

If you've taken a moment to assess the situation and still feel like you're genuinely being neglected by your friend, there are a few things you can do.

In our experience, we've found that friends rarely address this problem head-on. Instead, as their loved-up pal flakes on plans or grows more distant, the other friend just cops it on the chin. At best, they might fling a couple of passive-aggressive comments their way and stop extending so many social invitations. We've definitely done this and completely understand why it feels justified. If your friend never makes the effort to stay in touch or constantly dips out on plans because they're busy with their new flame, why would you want to bother inviting them? Sadly, we've also learned the hard way that palming your friend off without explanation doesn't help either of you.

Feeling like you're losing a friend is a crushing form of heartbreak in itself. So it's completely valid if you're in your feels and worry the friendship is slipping away. Instead of sending the 'k' text back when they say they can't make drinks on Friday, it's better to actually talk to your friend. This doesn't have to be a confrontation; it's best approached gently and from a place of understanding. Like all difficult conversations, this is one that should be done in person or over the phone if possible to avoid the misunderstanding of tone that's common over text or DM.

If you're feeling fired up, don't bring it up in the moment. Instead, give yourself a minute (even better, sleep on it) and broach the conversation when you're feeling calmer. Explain to your friend that you miss them and feel like you haven't spent as much time with them since they entered the relationship. You can empathise with them and explain that you're happy for them (if you genuinely are), but be clear that you'd really like to spend more time with them. To keep you both accountable, give yourselves a cute little goal to spend time together at least once a month (or however often you'd like, it's obvi up to you!). For example, you could reserve every third Sunday morning of the month for grabbing coffee and going for a walk together. We're also big fans of habit stacking: ticking off errands while having social time. For example, you could go to a market every weekend to pick up your fresh produce together or join the same gym so you can talk shit while closing your rings. Whatever you decide, it's going to be more productive for your friendship than avoiding the situation and letting the problem snowball.

This is also a good time to bring up any faults of your own, such as distancing yourself from the friendship out of spite or frustration. That way you're owning up to your part in what has happened, and your friend won't feel completely attacked.

You should also prepare yourself. It's very unlikely that your friend will smile and say 'Thanks for pointing out that I've been such a dud friend lately!' They'll probably get a little defensive or feel embarrassed or hurt. That's why packing this message in a shit sandwich, including your own shortcomings and a solution, can come in handy.

What happens if you haven't had this conversation, and your friend's relationship has blown up in their face and they've reached out to you for help? Consider the timing: if your friend is in the midst of heartbreak it probably isn't the best time to say 'I told you so' or point out that they haven't been a stand-up friend of late. If you care about your friend, put your pride aside and be there for them. Not only does your friend need you right now, but it's also a good opportunity to repair your bond. Invite them for a sleepover to watch cheesy movies and cry on the couch together. Encourage them to join in on group activities with other friends. Send them texts or give them a buzz if you haven't heard from them in a few days.

Once the wounds aren't so raw, you can say that you've really enjoyed spending more time with them lately. You can use that to springboard into explaining that you had been feeling a little neglected when they were dating their ex. Since the relationship is over now, it might be tempting to sweep the issue under the rug and pick up the friendship as normal. But it's important to share how you're feeling, not only to get things off your chest but also to give your friend some perspective before they enter their next relationship. By being honest, fingers crossed they'll be conscious of that and make more of an attempt to balance their friendships and romantic relationships in future.

When your friends and partner don't get along

Funnily enough, we both navigated this tricky terrain.

When we met, Sal was well and truly committed to Chris, while Al was post break-up and flirting with a co-worker. This turned into a two-year relationship followed by Al getting her heart broken and living on Sal's couch for a week. There were tears, *Friends* marathons and a multitude of face masks. But the relationship didn't properly end there; it was followed by two more years on and off, which had Sal wanting to rip her own hair out.

During those years we learned a *lot* about our friendship. We disagreed often, but by the end of it the most important lesson we *did* agree on and want to teach everyone is: do not sleep with your co-workers.

The day Al finally told Sal she'd been seeing her ex again, Sal cried. Not because she was mad (well, maybe a bit), but because she worried she hadn't given Al the space she needed to tell her. Plus, she was heartbroken over what she saw as a step back in Al's progress in getting over this relationship.

For the first time in our friendships we had to learn how to navigate something serious we didn't agree on. We're not talking about a Team Edward or Team Jacob situation here. We're talking about a disagreement that would probably be make-or-break for a lot of friends.

Sal didn't always dislike Al's on-again, off-again partner. There was a time the three of us would hang out most Fridays, drinking and giggling. But as the cracks in the relationship began to show and Al began to shed tears, Sal, not to any fault of her own, began to want better for her bestie. When you're the friend who is the sounding board when your mate needs to vent about their partner, it gets harder and harder to look past the issues and be happy for them in the relationship. Unlike your friend who is in love and therefore more likely to look past the red flags, you're not wearing the same rose-coloured glasses. Sometimes the hardest thing is suspecting your friend is making a mistake, but giving them the space to learn the lesson for themselves.

Our friendship meant a hell of a lot to us both, which is why we were able to see that we were going to disagree on the matter, and that was okay. The experience showed us that we can make it through anything. We're allowed to do things our friend doesn't necessarily like or agree with. It doesn't mean we don't respect each other's opinion or right to make our own decisions about our own lives.

Sal also realised if she wanted Al to talk to her about what was going on in her life, she needed to give her an open space free of judgement.

We can all probably think of a friend whose partner we are less than fond of. It can be disheartening, sad and frustrating, but letting things run their course is often the best thing we can do—for our friend, and ourselves.

A note from Sal

'Sally hates everyone's partners.' This was my reputation for a long time among my friends. To be honest, it probably still is a little bit. While I wouldn't say it's entirely true (I've loved many of my friends' partners over the years), I do have incredibly high standards for who my friends are dating and I'm not afraid to voice my opinions.

I would say this is a pretty universal experience. Your friend, who is an intelligent, hilarious and beautiful 10/10, starts dating someone who is a 3/10 on a good day. To paraphrase Greta Gerwig: your friend is everything. Their partner is just Ken.

You don't have to love your friend's partner. They're dating them, not you. But it is nice to see your friend thriving romantically with someone who loves, supports and builds them up as much as you do. I think it is your duty as their friend to have their best interests at heart, and sometimes that requires an uncomfortable conversation if you genuinely think their partner is treating them poorly or holding them back from their full potential.

How you have this conversation is a delicate dance, though. In the past, my approach was about as subtle as a brick. Some of the moments I'm not so proud of include rolling my eyes any time my friend uttered their partner's name, exclaiming 'What the fuck are you doing here?' if their ex showed up, or just straight bailing on social gatherings if I knew my friend's partner was going to be there. While admittedly devilishly fun at times, this tactic was not the way to go. I found that my friends were more likely to resent me, rather than respect me. Rather than listening to my advice, they'd hide details from me out of fear of me saying 'I told you so' when they just needed someone to vent to.

However, that doesn't mean that you have to lock your mouth and throw away the key. There's nothing worse than breaking up with someone, airing your grievances and having your mates come back with, 'Oh, yeah, I never liked them.' Like, WTF? Where was this information when I was dating the person?

The other side is that your friend shouldn't rely on you to be their emotional punching bag to trauma dump on if they're never going to take action to change their situation. This kind of exchange isn't healthy for anyone long-term. It can be very emotionally draining if you're the friend who is expected to constantly give out advice that is never followed through on. I would get super annoyed when my friends ignored my counsel, then came back to me later wanting more advice or a shoulder to cry on when their partner had treated them like shit again. Like, what do you mean you didn't follow my carefully curated step-by-step plan to dump their arse? That said, you can't control your friends' relationships, and they don't actually have to follow your advice just because you dished it out.

I'm always happy to listen to my friends' minor gripes about their relationships. Sometimes you need to be there for your friend when they want to bitch about their partner's inability to close drawers all the way.

For anything more than that, though, I now follow the three times rule. Let's say my friend keeps going back to their ex. I will allow myself to have three serious conversations with this friend. During these conversations, I'll listen and provide genuine advice on what I think they should do. If my friend doesn't do anything to remove themselves from this toxic cycle, by the fourth conversation I'll explain that I can't continue to be their friend slash therapist. In the past, this conversation has gone something like this:

'I will always be here for you, especially if things get really bad. However, I can no longer be the person you vent to about your partner. This has become extremely emotionally draining for me and it isn't helpful or healthy for anyone. I genuinely want you to be happy and I don't think this person is going to help you achieve that. However, it's your life and I respect that you're the only one who can make these decisions for yourself.'

Of course, this rule doesn't apply if your friend is in a genuinely toxic, abusive or dangerous situation. If that's the case, you should be doing everything you can to help your friend through and out of this relationship including helping them find and connect with the available services and support.

The three times rule is a healthy boundary to put in place in your friendship, and I truly believe it has helped save some of my friendships. Not only is the constant back-and-forth not good for your mental health, you could be enabling your friend to continue this cycle by being the emotional support blanket for them. These types of conversations can also lead to resentment building in a friendship, or even a big fight. Instead, my friends now know they can rely on me for support, but that they also have to be adults and deal with the consequences of their choices. It also means that if and when relationships do turn to shit, I actually have the emotional battery to be there for my friends.

Dear Sal and Al

My ex-boyfriend and I broke up about six months ago, but we often socialise in the same circles. He recently reached out asking to get a coffee. I'm not sure if I miss the relationship or his companionship as a friend. Is it possible to be friends with an ex, or am I just asking for trouble?

Trying to navigate the terrain with an ex who is still in your life is tricky. You have to unlearn and relearn how to interact with each other. There are often lots of emotions involved, whether your break-up was a mutual decision or an absolute dumpster fire. Plenty of people find themselves struggling with this predicament, ourselves included.

We always say that some time apart is necessary after parting ways with your significant other. It doesn't matter who broke up with whom or how it happened—in the immediate aftermath, you need to relearn how you navigate your life, and this requires a clean break.

Many people rely on their ex to help them through a break-up. Sending texts such as, 'Hope you're doing okay' or 'How are you feeling?' can be common practice.

Stop this.

If there is one thing we know for absolute certain, it's that your ex cannot coach you through your break-up. We know this may be hard to accept.

After every break-up you need to take time to check in with yourself and evaluate how you feel. Only then can you even approach the thought of having a platonic relationship with someone you've dated.

Sometimes when people ask the question 'Can you be friends with an ex?' they're really just looking for someone to give them the green light to hang out with their ex, even though they know it's the wrong decision. Al can tell you firsthand that spending time with an ex-partner too soon after a break-up is only going to lead to a delayed, painful and prolonged heartbreak. Being 'friends' with her ex in an on-again, off-again relationship not only had a negative effect on her, but also on her friendships.

We think the first and most important thing to consider when you're contemplating being friends with an ex is whether you can be honest with yourself.

You're not alone, unhinged or weird for wanting to be friends with an ex. This person knows you intimately, and in some way ending a relationship with a romantic partner is also ending a connection with your best friend. Whether you dated for a few months or years, you shared an important connection. You learned about each other's likes and dislikes and developed chemistry. Cutting the cord is fucking hard. A gap opens up in your life that you immediately want to fill and it feels like the easiest way to do so is by slotting them back in there.

Attempting to be friends with an ex can be like drinking milk a few days after its expiration date. You know it's past its time; at best it'll be a bit weird, and at worst you'll be crying, shitting and throwing up.

Ultimately, whether to be friends with someone you were once romantically involved with is an individual decision. However, there are a few factors that can illuminate whether you're potentially ready.

The idea of them with someone else doesn't make you want to heave

We're not saying you need to watch them make out with someone else and feel absolutely nothing. You're still a human who had feelings for this person. However, you do need to be okay with them moving on, dating, flirting with others and being intimate with someone who isn't you. If the very thought of those things makes your tummy start doing backflips like Simone Biles in the Olympics, friendship is not on the cards for you.

You miss their company, not the hungover cuddles or frequent sex

We once had a work friend, Riley, who broke up with their partner because they were seriously over it. They would complain about their partner at most morning coffee runs, no longer wanted to be intimate with them and even moved out before officially cutting the cord.

They were well and truly *done* being in that relationship.

However, after a few months of living the single life and their ex-partner moving on, they started to go backwards. At every after-work drinks, Riley would get very upset about how much they missed their ex, but when you dissected what they were 'missing' it wasn't actually their ex as a person. They were simply feeling lonely.

Ask yourself, do you genuinely miss your ex-partner, or do you miss the security, convenience and desire of a relationship? Answer honestly.

The relationship ended on respectful terms (not like in a Netflix rom-com)

Thankfully, this question can be answered simply: yes or no. If your relationship ended in a big dramatic blow-up that puts *Gossip Girl*'s Chuck and Blair to shame, it's time to completely shut the door and give the key to your bestie to throw into a bottomless pit.

As you can see, there isn't a one-size-fits-all answer to the question of whether you should be friends with your ex. But there is one consistent key: time.

After every break-up you need to take time. Whether you want to be friends in the future or not you need to step away and take off your rose-coloured glasses before you can have a level head and approach the situation objectively.

And remember, if you have to force it, it's probably shit.

Lots of love,

Sal and Al

Now for the reverse: your romantic partner doesn't like your friends. You may think that if your partner doesn't love your friends like you do, that's a deal-breaker, right? Not necessarily. Sometimes personalities don't mesh and that's okay. Let's say your best friend is a natural-born extrovert who lights up every room, whereas your partner is more introverted and prefers to take on the wallflower role. It's pretty understandable that they might not get on like a house on fire. If that's the case, your partner shouldn't be expected to spend every weekend with your best friend. However, they should be willing to spend time with them in instances where it supports you and a friendship that makes you happy.

Sometimes your partner may genuinely dislike one of your friends because they have your best interests at heart. They're not as invested in the friendship as you are, so they may be able to view your friendships more objectively than you can. For example, your partner may be able to pick up that one particular friend is regularly putting you down as a 'joke', which is something you may have brushed off as part of their personality.

It's important to use your best judgement and follow your gut feelings here. If a friendship isn't good for you, you usually know this deep down and it won't take your partner pointing it out for you to notice. Your partner's opinion may reaffirm how you've always secretly felt, but it probably won't be a totally revolutionary idea.

If your partner is pointing out alleged shortcomings in your friends that you don't agree with, or they are encouraging you to distance yourself from all your friends, that's not a good sign. It could be a red flag that you're in a controlling relationship and your partner is feigning concern about your friendships to isolate you. Sadly, we have both witnessed this happen. At the end of the day, you're an adult and should be able to choose who you spend your time with.

If your partner tells you you're spending too much time with your friends and not enough time with them, reflect on how you've been spending your time and (again) trust your gut, and the evidence. If you regularly spend every weekend socialising with friends and don't make room for quality time with your partner, they may have a point. However, if you catch up with a friend every Saturday morning for coffee or go out for a once a week girls' night, that's totally healthy in our opinion. If you do feel like you've been prioritising your friends over your romantic partner, it's worth having a conversation with your significant other about how they're feeling. Then ask them what you can do to help them feel like a more valued part of your life—whether it's a weekly date night, inviting them along to more group social gatherings or going on double dates with your friends and their partners.

If you're spending all of your spare time with your friends because you don't have the desire to spend time with your romantic partner, perhaps it's time to reflect on the future of the relationship.

On the flip side, what if your partner is constantly ditching you for *their* mates? Well, it's important to self-reflect. Ask yourself if they're really spending too much time with their friends or if you're being a little too needy. We're the first to admit to sometimes being a bit sooky when our boyfriends make plans without us. Every Friday, when Sal's boyfriend is about to leave for his weekly boys' night, she jokingly begs him to stay home and spend the night in with her instead. However, if your partner is genuinely spending most of their spare time with their mates and making no effort to prioritise quality time with you, you need to have a conversation with them. Explain that you're not feeling prioritised and would love to spend more time together one-on-one. Whether it's booking a weekend away or making a goal to spend every Sunday together, set a concrete plan and see if things improve. If they don't and you continue to play second fiddle to their mates, we think you know what to do.

When the lines get blurry: falling in love with a friend

You can't plan who you fall in love with. If you could, many of the world's problems would be solved. While it can be like playing with fire, falling for a friend is not that surprising. You likely enjoy spending time together, have similar interests and mutual friends, and maybe even off-the-charts chemistry. All solid foundations for a romantic relationship, no?

We don't have a hard-and-fast rule about dating friends, but we also don't encourage you to start hooking up with your friends willy nilly. We have both witnessed friendships transition into something more. Sometimes this works out, and sometimes it doesn't. A lot of Al's romantic relationships started as a slow burn: getting to know each other as friends and easing into the relationship.

If you do catch the feels, we advise that you approach with caution. If you think it's lust rather than love and the fling will burn bright and fast, it's worth considering how this could impact the future of your friendship. Are you both mature enough to move on and return to being platonic mates without compromising your friendship? Will it cause a rift in your friendship group? Is it likely that either of you will become jealous if the person moves on and strikes up a romance with someone new?

A note from Al

I've been in a situation where the line between friendship and romance became blurry—with one of my best friends, no less. I regret that we crossed that line.

I'd been dating on and off, and felt like everyone I'd been meeting was an absolute dud. I was having drinks with my friend, complaining to him in the melodramatic way featured in basically every rom-com. 'Why do all guys suck?' I whined.

I don't know why or how, but on this night the vibe shifted. We got flirty. (I'm lying. I do know why, and it rhymes with shmodka shlime shoda.) We ended up kissing and it was weird, but then kind of hot, but then weird again.

We started texting and saying we'd go on a date, but I'd always find a reason to reschedule.

The spark just wasn't there. I wanted it to be, so much. He made me laugh, he listened, he was kind and sexy and all the things I'd want to date, but just not *it*.

We ended up playing a game of hot potato for a few months: just friends, more than friends, just friends, more than friends. The back-and-forth wasn't fair to him, but I didn't know whether or not I felt romantic feelings for him.

In the end, we had to call it. And much to my regret, we never made it back to 'just friends'.

We'd made it weird.

While some people can hook up with a friend once or twice and have it be as uneventful as grabbing your Vegemite toast in the morning, there's always the risk you can't go back.

> I wanted to be friends, he wanted to be more, so we ended up being nothing. We still speak here and there, but with an understanding of distance.
>
> If you feel the lines blurring with a friend, think hard about whether you want to risk the friendship for the possibility of more. Some of the most beautiful relationships can be built from friendship, but some of the strongest friendships can be lost this way, too.

In a perfect world, our romantic relationships and friendships would always coexist in harmony. Sadly, we don't live in a perfect world. However, ensuring we aim for a healthy balance between our romantic and platonic relationships will help both us and the people in our lives feel more fulfilled.

Moving away from the idea that your friendships and romantic relationships are in competition with one another can also help. Instead, consider how the relationships in your life can complement each other, and place value on all of the connections you have with those you love.

FRIENDSHIP DATES

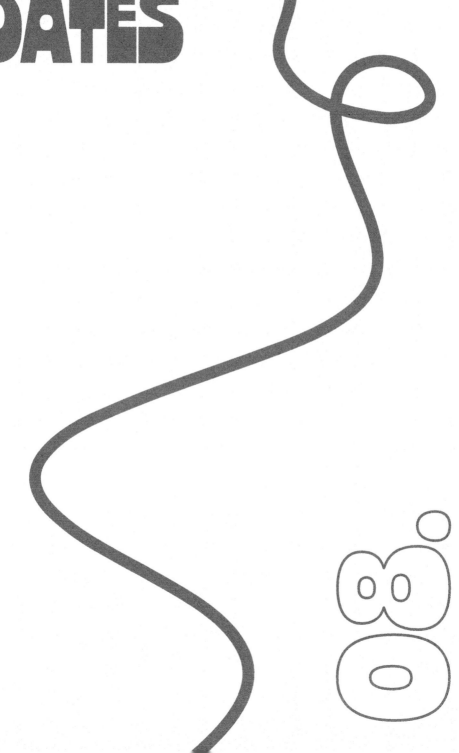

80

A friendship date is an actively planned session of quality time with mates. Not only are friendship dates healthy for your relationships, they're healthy for you. They serve as a way to detach from the world and any stressors that may be affecting you. Spending intentional time with your meaningful connections allows you to get back in touch with the things that really matter in life.

Friendship dates can take on many forms. They can be as simple as a coffee date or as outlandish as you want them to be. Ideally, you'll base them around something that you and your friend (or friends) enjoy, and see them as opportunities to spend some good ol' quality time together.

If you're short on ideas, let us elucidate to help get your creative juices flowin'.

Friendship dates that don't break the bank

Over the years we've had quite a few chicks ask us how to deal with different financial situations and priorities within friendships. People either spend money they don't have to join in on an expensive social event out of peer pressure, or they feel like they're always missing out by sticking to their financial boundaries. We totally get that this can be a really tricky spot to be in. It's so important to respect your friends' decisions when it comes to their finances. So, here are some friendship date ideas that won't hurt your (or your mate's) wallet.

Sunset picnic

Sunsets aren't just for romantic dates. Putting a picnic blanket down at your favourite lookout, beach or park to take in the sunset is also a super cute date idea for friends. Go to the supermarket and grab some crackers paired with whatever cheese and dips are on special. Bonus points if you bring your favourite bottle of cheap (but delish) wine. It's a good opportunity to slow down and reflect on your day while taking in the beautiful view. Plus, golden hour is the best time to snap some cute piccies with your best friend.

Hot girl walk

Get your 10,000 steps and some quality one-on-one time with a friend. It costs literally zero dollars to do and is a super-easy way to catch up on each other's lives. Plus, we swear that some of the juiciest conversations with your friends go down on a walk.

Not only is it good for your social life, walking is great for your mind and body. Research has found that ten minutes of walking every day can knock sixteen years off your biological age by midlife. Plus, exercise helps give your brain a boost of our fave neurotransmitters, dopamine and serotonin. Everyone's always talking about the runner's high, but post-walk brain chemicals are definitely a thing.

So put on your matching activewear set, grab your emotional support water bottle and your mate, and get walkin' and talkin'.

BYO dinner party

Even without set menus and expensive cocktails, dinners out with friends can be an expensive exercise. Instead, invite your friends to your house and ask everyone to bring a dish for a big potluck-style dinner party. So that you don't end up with a table full of desserts (unless that's by design), assign specific courses to specific friends: from entrees to mains, desserts and drinks.

It'll be a fun surprise seeing what everyone whips up, and way cheaper than eating out. Plus, you don't have to rush out because there's another booking, and you won't get charged a late fee because of that one mate who is incapable of arriving on time. (It's us. We're that mate.)

A note from Al

Taco Tuesday has such a special place in my heart.

When I lived with my housemate Sidnee, we and our fabulous adopted son (aka friend who didn't live with us), Jack, would do regular Taco Tuesdays. It didn't matter what had happened that day or whether we were finishing work late. We got there when we got there, because attendance was voluntarily compulsory.

On multiple occasions one of us would have had a rough day. During this time I was working for one of the worst managers I've ever had, the type of manager who could never decide how they wanted things, which led to me doing the same task multiple times and never quite feeling good enough. I was bone tired and frustrated, and sometimes the last thing I felt like doing was socialising.

I would come home bawling my eyes out, but within an hour, two hours max, I would be giggling into a rosé at some stupid thing Jack and Sidnee were doing to cheer me up.

These nights meant the absolute world to me. We didn't watch TV or sit on our phones. We poured wine, occasionally made tacos if we didn't get too drunk, and just spent time together. After a few drinks we'd start reading tarot cards as if we had any clue how to, followed by a Lipsync For Your Life battle to our favourite Kesha songs. We did, however, have to ban these when Sidnee tried to do a death drop and nearly ripped off her entire toenail. She then spent the rest of the night screaming when Jack tried to wash it under water and complaining because he put the sticky bit of the bandaid on her wound.

These nights put the scales back into place. Whenever we were upset about an ex, had a fight with our family or had the most cooked day at work, we always came back to the real things that mattered in life.

Because we're put on this earth to have fun and love people and that's exactly what we did every Tuesday night, drinking wine and, sometimes, eating tacos.

Friendship dates that make you try something new

Friendships can act as a safety net. They give you the comfort to try new things and lessen the fear of looking stupid, silly or feeling alone. They also give you the encouragement to step out of your comfort zone and try new things because, hey, you get to try it together! There's no need to be embarrassed when you've got your bestie there to help you laugh it off if things do go a bit south. One time in New York, we were dancing on the Coyote Ugly Bar. Yes, the one from the movie. We were doing our best to try (and failing) to be sexy while up on this bar and literally not one person gave a shit. It was hilarious. Until Al tried to do a sexy hair flick and absolutely smacked her head on a pipe in the roof. Sal, not missing a beat in her iconic dance moves, just said 'Shake it off' and kept on going. So that's exactly what Al did too. We're not saying you need to get on top of a bar and shake it, but we promise you that when you try new things and go out of your comfort zone with a friend you'll make some absolutely killer memories.

Exercise class

Trying a new exercise class can be super intimidating, and sometimes you need an emotional support buddy to help you get through the door. According to an Indiana University study, people who worked out separately at the gym had a 43 per cent dropout rate, while those who went to the gym in pairs only had a 6.3 per cent dropout rate. In a different study, participants were asked to hold a plank position for as long as they could.

Compared to people who were planking alone, those in pairs held the position for 200 per cent longer.

Having a workout buddy gives you the accountability you need to show up. It can also give you the confidence to try something new. There's something quite comforting about glancing at your mate in sheer panic while you're mid-move on a Pilates reformer. Plus, you can grab a coffee and sweet treat after to celebrate pushing yourselves out of your comfort zones.

Alphabet date

Alphabet dates are maybe the cutest friendship date idea ever. Weekly, monthly or however regularly you damn well please, you plan a date starting with a letter from the alphabet. For example, A = art gallery, B = brewery tour, C = camping. From A to Z, you take turns to plan friend dates, ticking off your personal friendship bucket list in the process.

Not only will it help shake up your usual Sunday brunch at the same cafe routine, it's also an amazing way to try new things and enjoy new experiences with your friend. Sure, things may get tricky when you get to Q and X, but the challenge is part of the fun. Plus, because you're taking turns deciding what to do, it means that one friend isn't always responsible for initiating all of the plans.

Friendship dates when you have little social battery

When your social battery is completely zapped, it's often best to spend time blowing off steam alone. But, sometimes, low-key time with good friends is exactly what you need to give that battery a little charge.

Movie night

Honestly, movie nights are an elite and underrated friendship date when you couldn't be fucked using any brain cells. Beyond choosing the movie and session time, there's very little decision-making involved. Plus, since it's frowned upon to gasbag in the cinema, it's the perfect excuse to spend time with a friend without draining your social battery. It's not completely anti-social, though: the occasional knowing glance, mutual giggle and tear shed is enough to have a little bonding moment mid-movie. Plus, if you're anything like us, the right film can become a springboard for personal jokes, sentimental moments or spellbinding soundtracks that bind your friendship even closer.

If you don't have a casual $3000 to throw at movie tickets and a candy bar combo (that's roughly how much it costs these days, right?), you can always host the movie night at home. Chuck on your comfiest pyjamas, order some takeaway and snuggle on the couch together. If you're both feeling a little physically and emotionally drained, queue up your favourite comfort films that you've watched 73 times and take next to no energy to enjoy.

• •

20 best films to watch on a friend date

① *The Breakfast Club*
② *Thelma and Louise*
③ *Now and Then*

④ *Clueless*

⑤ *Suddenly 30*

⑥ *10 Things I Hate About You*

⑦ *The Sisterhood of the Travelling Pants*

⑧ *The Intern*

⑨ *Mamma Mia*

⑩ *Pretty Woman*

⑪ *Ferris Bueller's Day Off*

⑫ *Mean Girls*

⑬ *Romy and Michele's High School Reunion*

⑭ *Sex and the City* movie

⑮ *The Perks of Being a Wallflower*

⑯ *Love, Simon*

⑰ *Legally Blonde*

⑱ *Sing Street*

⑲ *Beaches*

⑳ *Uptown Girls*

• •

Pamper day

Couples massage anyone? But, seriously, a day of pampering could do you and your friend wonders if you're both feeling a little burned out by life. At our old job, we would frequently book in midday manicures to get coordinating nail art on our lunch break. Some of the conversations we'd have in those nail chairs were more healing than therapy, let us tell ya. We also spent an entire week in Bali getting massages at the same time. And aside from the one flower bath that had a leech in it, it was worth every cent.

So whether it's a blowout with a glass of champagne or a relaxing DIY facial, book a pamper day with your bestie and you'll both emerge sparkling new and ready to take on the world.

Friendship dates that make you talk

As much as we love sitting in silence with our best friend, it's really important to *talk* to your friends. It's also important to go beyond the same three topics that you absolutely love complaining or gossiping about or deep diving into. When you talk about the same things every time, you don't give yourselves space to learn new things or disagree in a healthy manner.

Conversation card game

Conversation card games might sound boring in theory but, trust us, they're so fun. You don't have to use any brain power to think of juicy questions, and can instead put all your energy into thinking of interesting and fun answers and listening to what your friends have to say.

We love conversation card games so much we brought out our own range called Rich Conversations. As a sneak peek, here are some fun questions to ask your friends at your next happy hour or sleepover:

- Would you rather unwavering support or brutal honesty always?
- If you could *Freaky Friday* yourself with someone for one day, who would it be and why?
- What's a disgusting habit you don't think is that gross?

- If you could choose a fictional universe to live in, which would it be and why?
- What's the strangest thing you've ever seen?
- If you had 24 hours with zero consequences, how would you spend your day?

Book club

We may be biased because we absolutely adore reading, but there is nothing better than fangirling over a good book with your bestie. Bonus points if it's a smutty fairy book with an enemies-to-lovers plot point that you can giggle over.

Daytrip

Daytrips are key to making memories. Even the trips where everything seems to go wrong will still end up as memories you look back on and smile about.

Once we were driving on a three-hour road trip to Hunter Valley wine country and we got so lost we decided to get matching tattoos. Did it make sense? No. Do we love the memory, and do we smile every time we look at our tattoos? Yes.

Al once went on a day hike with her boyfriend and besties Sean, Pia and Anna. They decided to go to the Royal National Park and hike to the Figure Eight Pools. The only problem was the hike includes about 981,000 billion stairs, and Al was disgustingly hungover. The entire hike she daydreamed of spooning a brown paper bag holding a cheeseburger and frozen Coke. However, her friends rallied around her while she climbed the stairs within the clutches of death (we're not joking; we're in awe of anyone who has done that hike). Everyone was there with water bottles, words of encouragement and jokes to make the pain more bearable. To this day we still talk about this hike, and even though Al would never do it again it is one of her favourite memories.

Explore new places with your friends. Don't be worried about whether it's 'worth it' or if it doesn't go exactly as expected. Sometimes these are the memories we end up cherishing and smiling about the most.

Shopping session

Shopping with your friends is absolute heaven, and you can't tell us otherwise. Getting retail therapy and having your own 2000s movie montage moment trying on outfits together? Yes, please. There are plenty of opportunities for icebreaking, so it's a great way to catch up with a friend and talk.

We especially love shopping at vintage stores, op shops and markets together. There's nothing like the thrill of finding the perfect vintage top with a pal who will validate all of your impulse purchases. It's a bonding experience like no other.

Since shopping with friends mostly consists of touching random items, saying 'This is cute!' and then walking away without buying the thing, it's not always a super expensive activity either.

Travelling: the ultimate friendship date

Travelling with friends creates a bond like nothing else. Exploring new cities, eating amazing food and almost biting each other's heads off because you can't read street signs in a foreign language: these are all things that can make for core memories. Visiting new places solo or with a partner also has its own advantages, but everyone should go on a big adventure with their mates at least once if they can.

The memories you make while travelling are ones that last. There's something incredible about sharing an experience that puts you out of your comfort zone, exposes you to new ways of living and creates lifelong memories with a friend. These trips can turn into traditions or the folklore of your friendship that you'll look back on fondly when you're old and grey. Even before you step on a plane, the whole process of booking flights, swapping recs in the group chat and planning your itinerary is so fun.

But similar to living together, travelling with mates can be a make-or-break kinda situation. Not all friends make for great travel companions. If one friend likes to plan out everything from breakfast spots to bathroom breaks and the other likes to see where the day takes them, this can cause issues. The keys to a successful vacay with friends are communication, understanding and patience. Remember that this isn't just your holiday, it's also your friends'.

That said, sometimes different personality traits *can* come in handy while travelling with friends. We're taking you back to 2019 and our first time travelling together. It was a work trip to America that saw us conquer LA, Seattle and New York. The entire experience was amazing, but it was a whirlwind with multiple conferences, a work presentation to the entire office and many big nights out. We took shots at the Saddle Ranch in

West Hollywood (where we ran into Jack Nicholson, a highlight of our lives) and missed flights in Seattle.

While we're very compatible for the most part, there are some differences in how we like to travel. Al can whip up a holiday itinerary spreadsheet like no one's business and prefers to balance out the trip with a mix of relaxing and active experiences. Sal's severe case of FOMO means she prefers to pack every waking second with something in the itinerary.

Three weeks into our trip we'd had so much fun, but we were fucking exhausted. We only had a few days left, but our social batteries were starting to shoot off sparks. It was also the middle of a brutal heatwave in New York. We'd finished a long day in the office and were feeling a little dusty from the night before (surprise, surprise). Nevertheless, we went out for dinner with a friend at a beautiful restaurant in Little Italy. We had planned to hit up the infamous Lips drag bar that night. But after we'd eaten our weight in pasta and had a lie-down back in our room, Al looked to Sal and said, 'I don't know if I can do it.' Sal reminded Al that we had been looking forward to checking out this drag bar for weeks. Her theory was that we could sleep when we got back home to Sydney, but we may not have another chance to check out this drag bar any time soon. (The pandemic kicked in the following year so that theory wasn't wrong.)

After much hyping up, we changed outfits and were in a cab on our way to Lips. And thank fuck we were because it ended up being one of the best nights of our entire lives. Not only were the drag performers *incredible*, we made friends with one of the bartenders who served us good drinks and even better banter all night long. Before long, we were behind the bar with her and trying our hand at whipping up some cocktails.

Behind that bar in New York we tried a shot. We can't tell you what was in it, but we can tell you that we both immediately hurled after it. It's honestly one of the highlights of our friendship and a story we retell on the regular.

This is just one instance when travelling with friends with different travel styles has its silver linings. If we decided to stay at the hotel that night, we wouldn't get to tell the story of that one time we worked behind the bar at a drag club in the Big Apple.

Finding time to hang out with friends as an adult can feel like an impossible game of calendar Tetris at times. It may not be doable as much as you would like, but we encourage you to find the time to see, love and laugh with your people as often as you can. It doesn't have to be a four-hour hang—even a quick morning walk adds to your cup more than if you didn't bother.

LIFE LESSONS FROM ICONIC BESTIES

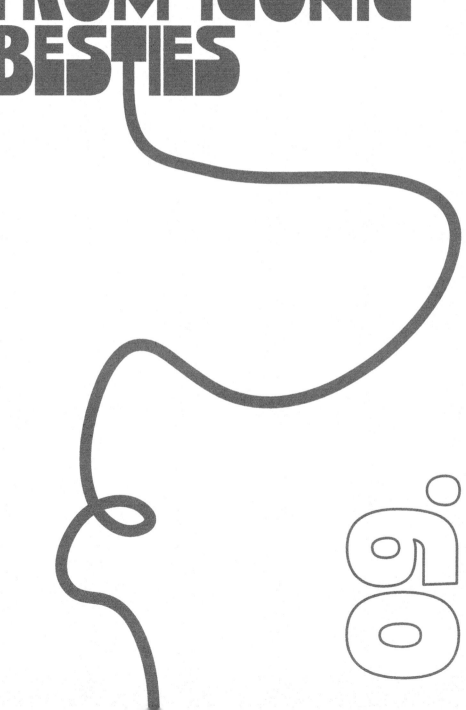

Pop culture has a *huge* impact on how we perceive friendships can and should look. Case in point: we're aware we've referenced *Sex and the City* approximately 300 times in this book so far (and we won't apologise for that). As two big pop culture nerds, we also consider many fictional characters as real friends and take in the lessons they've taught us with the same significance as we would an IRL mate.

Sometimes television, movies and iconic celebrity best friends can give us unrealistic expectations of what adult friendships can look like. Other times they can give us incredible perspective and sage advice that we can apply to our real-life relationships.

It would probably take a whole second book to share all of our favourites, so we've cherrypicked a select few life lessons from pop culture besties in the hope they'll help you view the friendships in your own life in a different light as well.

Joey and Chandler from *Friends*

LIFE LESSON: don't let money get in the way of true friendship.

As we've mentioned, our podcast listeners, the chicks, regularly send us their own life lessons. An incredibly common lesson we're sent is: *don't lend your friends money.*

Money is a topic that can split people down the middle. It can pull apart the very fabric of what was once a healthy friendship. And our social norms mean it can be very awkward to talk about. According to a 2021 survey from Insider, people would rather talk about current events, politics and relationships before discussing money with their friends.

The topic of friendship and money makes us think about the friendship between Chandler and Joey on the sitcom TV show *Friends*. Their friendship is completely underrated in our opinion. Monica and Rachel get a lot of hype, but we personally think the brotherly bond that Chandler and Joey share is pure wholesome bestie soulmate energy. We see a lot of ourselves in their dynamic, honestly.

At the time of writing this book, Matthew Perry, the actor who played Chandler, tragically passed away. People around the world, us included, were heartbroken by this. He genuinely felt like a real friend to us, even through a TV screen. We witnessed the heavy weight of this loss on the cast of *Friends*, which we think shows how genuine their connection was both on and off screen. It makes this show one of the most beautiful to learn from at any stage of life.

If you've never watched *Friends* or you need a refresher, Joey and Chandler are roommates and best pals. They bond over their pet chicken and duck and their two recliner chairs, and give the best hugs you've ever seen on a television set.

Chandler often supported his friend financially as Joey tried to make it as an actor. We're talking about forking out for the apartment furniture after they were robbed and covering the bill for Joey's acting headshots. Then, in season eight, episode 22 ('The One Where Rachel is Late') we learn exactly how much this friendship 'cost'. It turns out that Chandler has basically been paying for all of Joey's expenses since he moved to the city. After Chandler falls asleep in Joey's movie premiere, Joey decides to forgive him after calculating how much his mate has been paying for him.

It's a staggering amount. According to *Marie Claire*, Joey owes Chandler $120,760.

What the fuck, right?

Here's what we really love about Joey and Chandler's relationship, though: while we don't think you should *ever* be lending your friends thousands of dollars, money never got in the way of their friendship.

Lending cash to friends

Ask any accountant if you should lend your friend some cash and you'll get a pretty quick 'no' in response. In our experience, though, the decision about whether or not to lend a friend money depends on the friend you're lending to, the amount you're lending and whether you're comfortable never getting that money back. (Not because you definitely won't get it back, but it's a risk you take whenever you lend money to anyone— even a close friend.) If you can't 100 per cent trust that the person is going to be able to pay you back the money, you have your answer.

If you do have a friend who asks to borrow money and you are tossing up whether you want to, there are a few things to consider:

- Are they in debt?
- Do they have a family member who could help out?
- Is this an actual financial emergency or a 'nice to have'?

Also be aware that, when you lend your friend money, you'll probably become invested in their finances. When will they get their next paycheque? How did they afford to go to that bottomless brunch you saw them attending on Instagram Stories when they still owe you money?

If you do decide to lend your friend money, it's incredibly crucial to set boundaries and guidelines. Here are some tips:

- Make a checklist of questions you need answered before settling on an amount.
- Understand the exact amount of money you will loan them. Put a limit on this. You don't want friends borrowing money then coming back again to ask for more. Set a clear parameter of how much you'll lend them, and tell them it's capped.
- Set out a payment plan—a clear timeline that lists when and how you will be repaid. Figure out if they will repay you in one go or in instalments and, if so, how often those instalments will occur.

For us, we're always happy to cover our friends in small and casual amounts here and there. If Al gets dinner, Sal will buy the drinks the next time we're out. We don't pull hairs stressing about the $5 coffee we bought the other. We transfer cash to each other when we owe it, and don't take it personally if one of us accidentally forgets and needs a reminder. However, that's our financial situation and dynamic, which may not necessarily work for everyone. We don't blame you if you feel a little funny about money and friendships, especially if you've been burned before.

Income disparity in friendships

In *Friends* season two, episode five ('The One With Five Steaks and an Eggplant') the group shares a tension-filled dinner. The trouble arises because Monica, Chandler and Ross are ignorant of the fact that Joey, Rachel and Phoebe earn significantly less money than them; that dinners, drinks and concert tickets aren't as simple for their friends to splurge on. In the end, the 'high-income' friends offer to pay for the others, which translates as patronising rather than helpful. While they had the best of intentions offering to pay, friends aren't charity cases. On the other hand, should the lower-earning friends have felt pressured to spend more because the others could afford the bougie dinner?

Income or wealth disparity in friendships can cause hiccups. Sometimes it seems like our worth is measured next to a dollar figure, and when ours is lower than those we see around us it's hard to not feel down on ourselves. It can feel like a punch to the gut when we have to reply to the group chat and say, 'Sorry,

I can't afford that right now.' We may even start being left out if those who can afford more begin to exclude those who can't.

While it's easy to feel insecure about our money, we urge you to try not to be. Just like all insecurities in friendships, this issue needs to be talked about. Take the opportunity to be open and vulnerable with your friends. If you're scared your mates will judge you, it's time to rethink those friendships.

If your friends are inviting you to something that's out of your budget, your response can be simple. There are only two steps to it:

① Explain honestly why you can't go.
② Propose an alternative that does sit within your budget.

Here is a script you can use:

> Hey [friend], *thank you so much for inviting me but unfortunately I'm* [saving at the moment/tightening the purse strings/not able to afford that right now]. *Would you like to* [come over and join me for a *High School Musical* marathon] *instead?*

(We don't know anyone who could say no to a *High School Musical* marathon. No friend worth keeping, that's for sure.)

Respecting your friends' finances and being fair, no matter the difference between you, is the simplest way to navigate friendships and money. If you get a bill for a shared experience, don't immediately say 'Let's split it down the middle' when you know you had four cocktails and your friend had one glass of wine. If you're the friend who only had the wine, speak up. We know it may feel weird but it shouldn't be. Your true friends don't want you to have to eat plain rice for the rest of the month because you spent so much on drinks and dinner that you didn't even consume.

The bottom line is, true friends don't want you to spend money that you don't have, and you should never assume your friend's financial position. Just because you're willing to fork out $700 for VIP tickets to Taylor Swift, that doesn't mean they are.

When managing money and friendships, lead with empathy and finish with boundaries.

Mia and Lilly from *The Princess Diaries*

LIFE LESSON: your oldest friendships aren't always the best ones.

Ahhh, Mia and Lilly from the 2001 classic *The Princess Diaries*. Two lifelong best friends and social outcasts who find solace in the safety of their friendship. Their friendship is made up of girly giggles, mocking the mean popular kids and hanging out with Lilly's hot older brother Michael. Sounds like the perfect friendship, right?

When we watched this film growing up, we looked up to Mia and Lilly's relationship and thought exactly that. Yet when we rewatch it now, as adults . . . it feels almost like a betrayal to our younger selves to admit it, but Lilly kinda sucks. And by that we mean, she really fucking sucks.

Yes, she has her positive traits. She's an advocate. She sticks up for Mia when her classmates are being total dicks. And she encourages her when she's scared to debate in front of the class.

However, there are some big flashing warning signs that we can't ignore. She asks Mia when she's going to stop moping about her dad's death. To paraphrase Lilly: 'It has already been two months and you barely knew him. Get over it.' Girl, what the fuck?

Lilly also mocks Mia after she goes through one of *the* most iconic beauty makeovers in pop culture history and rocks up to school with a new haircut. Your majesty, Paolo is exhausted and so are we. Last but not least, she only gets on board with the news that Mia is secretly a princess once she realises she can use her for her internet chat show. C'mon now.

We're not the only ones who've noticed this, either. The internet is full of commentary from Millennial and Gen Z folks who have grown up and realised what a dud mate Lilly is. And we have a theory why this particular pop culture realisation has struck a chord with so many people.

It's because many of us grew up with that one friend who we've been close with *forever* but who is sometimes downright mean. The friendship isn't all bad; they're not always outwardly nasty. You get along well most of the time and share a lot of interests. There are moments when you're there for each other, and many of your favourite memories are shared with them. Something feels a little off about the friendship, but you put up with it anyway. Why? Because you've been friends forever. We totally get it.

While all is well between Mia and Lilly by the end of the movie when they're doing the robot dance at Mia's coronation ball, there are some good life lessons to take from their friendship. Just because you have a long history with a friend doesn't mean you should put up with their shitty behaviour. At one point Mia does stand up for herself and confronts Lilly about her bitterness, and this is a good lesson that sometimes confrontation can lead to a stronger friendship.

Cassie and Maddy from *Euphoria*

LIFE LESSON: don't fuck your friend's significant other, ex, crush . . . you get the point.

If you watched season two of *Euphoria*, you know the way this particular friendship betrayal rocked everyone to the core.

Don't get us wrong. It's completely okay and a normal experience to wake up after a late-night escapade and wonder, 'What was I thinking?' But it's not okay for that escapade to involve a friend's ex-partner.

Cassie and Maddy's friendship starts as wholesome as one can on a show like *Euphoria*. Seriously, most friends probably can't relate to buying molly at a pretzel stand followed by one friend having a big O on a carousel, but we don't judge.

These two were thick as thieves. Even when boys, school and other drama arose, they always had each other's back. When Cassie broke up with her first boyfriend, Maddy was there for her, and when Maddy had trouble with her parents and boyfriend (soon-to-be ex) Nate, Cassie supported her.

That's the thing: we're not talking about sleeping with the significant other of someone you've met in passing at parties or worked with four years ago. We're talking about *best* friends.

Maddy and Nate had an incredibly toxic relationship, with him even physically harming her during their relationship. It made us as viewers feel relieved when they broke up.

It's basically the number-one commandment of a friendship: when your bestie goes through a bad break-up, you show up with a voodoo doll in the shape of their ex, a list of cheesy movies and an audacious care pack of snacks that you couldn't finish even if you tried.

The days, weeks and months post break-up can be the most raw times in our lives—whether the relationship we're mourning was healthy or not. In these moments we turn to our friends to help us put what's been broken back together. They're the ones who encourage us to avoid snoop our ex's socials so we don't hurt our own feelings. They help distract us from the way our stomach drops when we think about our ex with another person.

If that 'other person' is also your best friend, you don't experience a heartbreak. You experience two.

Many people argue that the couple has broken up, so the best friend didn't do anything wrong—but, in our opinion, that's just an excuse to try to dodge blame. This was the hill Cassie tried to die on. That since Maddy and Nate had broken up, she hadn't betrayed her best friend.

Watching a friendship so close fall out over something as stupid as a mediocre man made for a hard watch. The affair goes on for an entire season, and many viewers held excitement and discomfort while waiting for the moment that Maddy would find out and dish out her valid retribution and sweet, sweet revenge.

Instead, we got the opposite. Instead of the dooming confrontation that we believed had been building all season long, we watched a betrayed and heartbroken now ex-best friend ask, 'Was it worth it?'

In front of viewers' eyes we watched a pair once inseperable become total strangers to one another. When the shock and anger faded away all that was left was disappointment, disloyalty and deception.

Of course, some cases are a lot less dramatic than this. We both know people who have dated a friend's ex and things worked out and there was zero drama involved. But if your friend loved this person or would feel hurt by you going there, proceed with caution. And if you do mess up, don't be a Cassie. Be honest and remorseful, and expect them to need time. It's okay to fuck up; it's even better to say sorry for it.

Romy and Michele from *Romy and Michele's High School Reunion*

LIFE LESSON: you'll find the best friendships when you're being true to yourself.

If, like us, you were a bit of a loser as an angsty teen, you know that finding your fellow outcasts can be a powerful set of armour. That's probably why we can relate so much to the 1997 cinematic classic *Romy and Michele's High School Reunion*. The film opens with our protagonists Romy and Michele, two kinda clueless besties who are both social outcasts at their high school. They're harassed and ostracised by the so-called cool kids in their grade, yet they seem blissfully unaware of their dismal position on the social ladder. Because they have each other, and that's enough.

Even beyond high school, a lot of us feel pressure to have a huge group of close friends. While there's nothing wrong with having a lot of friends, it's not the only sign of true friendship. As we covered in Chapter 4, quantity doesn't always equal quality. Like Romy and Michele, we'd rather have a few really solid ride-or-dies than a big group of fair-weather mates.

The premise of the film is that Romy and Michele are invited to their ten-year high school reunion. Even in their twenties, they're still best friends who now live together and exist in the world as an iconically dressed package deal. It's still Romy and Michele against the world, baby, and they're absolutely content with that.

That's until the pressure of showing up to their high school reunion kicks in. Suddenly their fabulous life of coordinated nylon outfits, slumber parties and mutual love for Madonna makes them feel inadequate. They decide they need to make up for ten years of lost time to prove that they are 'successful'. Rather than celebrating the amazing memories they've created together, they start fabricating stories about the relationships, career and other life goals that they think will impress the jerks from their high school. They veer away from the things that make them special and thus bond them, and it's here that cracks start to show in the friendship.

Given that the film concludes with a three-way interpretive dance to Cyndi Lauper's 'Time After Time', it might feel like we're taking this film a little too seriously. While it is incredibly camp and hilarious, it also has a beautiful message that at the end of the day you should always be unapologetically yourself. Not only is that where you find true contentment with your-self, it's also where you'll find your true friends. The ones who don't love you *despite* of all of your apparently weird quirks and interests, but *because* of them.

Romy and Michele's High School Reunion is a big fuck you to the pressure of being a social butterfly who floats between different friend groups. A fuck you to moulding your interests to whatever is popular. A fuck you to changing yourself to impress anyone else (especially the duds you went to high school with).

Lorelai and Rory from *Gilmore Girls*

LIFE LESSON: you can find true friendship within family.

Gilmore Girls largely revolves around the mother-daughter friendship between Lorelai and Rory Gilmore. In addition to our affinity with their caffeine addictions and love for lightning-speed shit-talking, there are *plenty* of life lessons about friendship that we've drawn from the Gilmores.

The most obvious is that it's actually cool to call your mum your best friend. Throughout the show, Rory is literally never ashamed to admit that her partner in crime is her mother. They exist in their own impenetrable fortress of friendship in which they happily spend almost all of their spare time together. They can also be earnest with one another and, *mostly*, openly tell each other everything (usually without too much judgement). While Lorelai occasionally has to pull rank, their relationship largely exists on a horizontal plane of respect rather than the traditional hierarchy many people had with their parents growing up.

A note from Sal

My mum and I have a similar dynamic to Lorelai and Rory. This took time to develop, though. I was always a mummy's girl growing up, but tough moments in life combined with teen angst definitely threw some curveballs at our relationship. Once I left high school, though, my mum and I truly bonded as adults. It now feels more like a friendship than a mother-daughter relationship at times. We share clothes, go to concerts together and can spend hours on the phone swapping television show recs and links to Spotify playlists.

While I will always turn to her for motherly advice when I need it (like how to get pasta sauce out of a new t-shirt), I'm grateful that my relationship with Mum has flowered into more of a friendship over the years.

However, just like any good friendship, Rory and Lorelai do occasionally call each other out. They don't always do this perfectly throughout the seasons (looking at you in season four, girls). But eventually, they move past their pride and have the tough conversations despite the potential strain it might put on their usual sunshine-and-rainbows relationship.

This show is a powerful reminder that you can have an earnest yet playful relationship with your family members. Rory and Lorelai's dynamic is something that we personally didn't figure out with our parents until we were well into adulthood. Before this it was more likely we saw our folks as a source of cringe rather than a place to find friendship. Looking back we can see that many of us spent our adolescence doing everything we could to avoid spending time with our parents.

As we grow older, while the age gap remains the same the emotional gap between us and our parents slowly but surely shrinks. We realise that this is also our parents' first run at life, and many of the things we rolled our eyes at or resented them for in the past were done either for our own good or as a result of our parents' very human flaws. We've both experienced this firsthand and have incredible friendships with our mums, which we feel extremely lucky to be able to say.

Siblings are often a similar situation. They can go from being your mortal enemy to someone you would go out of your way to spend time with. Wild, huh?

Because they're forced upon us, it can be easy to take our family members for granted. As we grow into adults, it can also be tricky to navigate our way out of the hierarchical structures we grew up with. But if we can move through that, our family members can grow into some of the most rewarding and genuine connections of all.

A note from Al

My mum wasn't always my best friend, for one main reason: she was my mum and I was a teenager. There were boundaries.

However, we were also very different people. My mum has always been good natured, gentle and patient. Meanwhile, I take after my father with his cheeky nature. Swearing is a form of endearment for me. My favourite jokes feature dark humour and self-deprecation. And sometimes I have about as much patience as a bull standing in front of a matador.

Mum was also an incredibly successful school principal, so growing up I always felt like she was quite strict. I'd get in trouble for wearing mascara to school, if my skirt was too short or for saying the word 'crap'.

The thing is, it's not our parents' jobs to be our best friends when we're teenagers. They need to find the balance between being someone we like and look up to while also being a respected authoritative figure.

Your mum isn't going to help you sneak out to see a boy when you're sixteen, but hopefully she will hold your hand when he breaks your heart. Your mum isn't going to get blackout drunk with you after your school formal, but hopefully she will make you Vegemite toast and orange juice when you're sick.

I have the utmost respect for Mum, Dad and all parents. It's a hard balancing act wanting your kids to genuinely like you but also needing to make decisions for them that won't necessarily be popular.

As I entered my twenties, the gap between mother-daughter relationship and best friend relationship started to become narrower. We started talking about things we hadn't previously, and it was as though we met each other in the middle of our personalities. We encouraged positive growth and understanding in each other. She helped me comprehend myself as an adult and I like to think I helped her let her hair down from time to time. We started enjoying glasses of wine together, which is how I inherited my 'ice with wine, always!' habit. We'd gossip about boys, and on the odd occasion Mum would swear, followed by a giggle that could only be compared to one of a naughty little girl doing something she knows she shouldn't.

I do also want to give a big shoutout to my dad, who is my partner in crime. He is the parent I have to thank for inheriting 99.9 per cent of the spicy flare in my personality.

I'm very lucky to think of both my parents as best friends in my life. I know this isn't an experience a lot of people can relate to, but if you can find a friend in family it's a great thing. Maybe it's the cousin who you see at Christmas and you know you're in for a good time. Maybe it's a grandparent who listens to you when no one else will. Or maybe you're like Sal, who quite literally found her soul sister in her sister.

You can also find family in all walks of life—they don't necessarily need to be blood relatives.

I think sometimes we overlook and undervalue the incredible friendships family members can provide us with. Just like friendships, it's not always perfect. There are fights, tears and occasional cries of 'Who ate my leftover pizza?!'

But we love 'em, nonetheless.

Eric and Otis from *Sex Education*

LIFE LESSON: don't ignore the differences between you and your friends just because it's hard to talk about.

We could write an entire book on the learnings and lessons found within the four glorious seasons of *Sex Education*. It's one of our favourite shows and we both sobbed through multiple episodes.

As much as we love Otis's goofy nature, he does have a bad habit of taking centre stage in not only his own life, but everyone else's too. His problems are always bigger, his success is always more exciting and he doesn't quite remember to check in with his friends or seek to understand what's going on in their lives.

This doesn't make us hate him or even dislike him because every character on *Sex Education* has their flaws. That's what makes the show such perfection. Except Aimee. Aimee is flawless and we should protect her at all costs.

Otis and Eric, along with a bunch of other students, are forced to enrol in a new school when their old high school shuts down. Previously, Eric and Otis were bonded as loveable outcasts—never fitting in and not necessarily trying to, since they had each other. However, at their new college, the tables flip and Eric quite easily and by happy accident falls in with the 'cool kids'. Eric also goes through a major journey with the battle between his queer sexuality and his faith—an internal battle that Otis knows nothing about, because he never asks. Eyeroll.

As much as we, like Otis, can get wrapped up in the messiness and chaos of our own world, we need to remember our friends have their lives, too. Even when our world can feel up in arms, it's not fair to drop our friends or trauma dump on them without checking in on how they're doing. If we're doing all the talking, it might be time for a little self-reflection—chances are we're unintentionally creating distance in our friendships, as no one ends up feeling understood.

In *Sex Education*, Otis feels as though Eric is ditching him for new friends, and Eric feels as though Otis doesn't seek to understand him or spend time together other than when it's convenient for Otis. The tension comes to a head when their tit-for-tat bickering evolves into a building fight. Another example as to why it's important to bring us tension in friendships before it hits boiling point. Eric finally brings up Otis's reluctance to discuss the very obvious differences in their lives—Eric as a black, queer, religious human, Otis as a straight, white human from a family with a higher socioeconomic status—and how these have built tension and caused them to drift apart. Eric wants Otis to recognise his privilege and make more of an effort to understand the tension points in Eric's life. Otis shuts the conversation down out of fear of addressing these differences, and the two agree (with tension still very much present) to take some time apart.

As we've already discussed in this book, if you don't give your friends enough airtime this will create a barrier between you, and if you don't seek to understand your friends on a deep level this will limit how meaningful the friendship can truly be. Refusing to address the differences between you and your friends is about as good a solution as burying your head in the sand.

Thankfully, we do see Otis come to his senses and shed his stubborn nature and inability to admit he's wrong. He confesses he was scared to address their differences and that his inability to discuss them stemmed from a fear of saying the wrong thing and upsetting Eric.

We shouldn't be afraid to have hard conversations with friends. It's not going to be something we jump at the opportunity to do, but knowing that we can talk about the hard things and still have the friendship at the end is the definition of a secure friendship.

Every time you have a difficult conversation and listen to each other, you walk away not only a better person but with a better understanding of your friendship, too.

FINDING YOUR SOULMATE

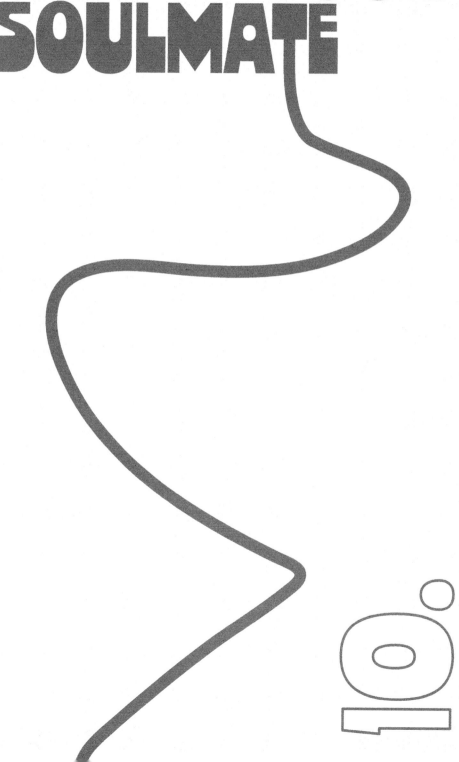

16.

The term 'soulmate' is usually one we reserve for romantic relationships. It conjures up images of couples who finish each other's sentences, of white dresses and wedding rings, of cute old couples we see walking hand in hand that make us cry into our iced coffees on our way to work. You know? Romance and all that jazz. However, we're firm believers that soulmates shouldn't be a label that's exclusive to romantic relationships. It applies to friendships, too.

So, what's the difference between romantic and platonic soulmates? 'Platonic soulmates are a very long-term, solid, trusting, and very satisfying relationship,' states clinical psychologist Meredith Fullers. 'There are three things people want in a relationship: one, passion (which includes sex and lust); two, intimacy; and three, commitment. It is the second two, intimacy and commitment, that a platonic soulmate offers us.'

A soulmate is someone who completes you. It's a person with whom you have an inexplicable, unshakable and magical connection. When you think of it like that, it seems naive and almost wasteful to use that label only for romantic partners.

Your soulmate is someone who seems to exist on the same wavelength as you. You know when you're in a group situation and you and your friend have a telepathic, in-depth conversation just in one glance? That's a soulmate connection. Or what about when you two aren't even together but you can sense something is off, so you send them a text to check in only to hear that they're experiencing the worst day ever? That's some soulmate shit right there.

The joy of platonic love

The term 'platonic soulmate' actually derives from the Greek philosopher, Plato. Plato wrote:

According to Greek mythology, humans were originally created with four arms, four legs and a head with two faces. Fearing their power, Zeus split them into two separate parts, condemning them to spend their lives in search of their other halves.

What's interesting is that Plato's definition of a soulmate isn't outwardly romantic. He continues to explain:

. . . and when one of them meets the other half, the actual half of himself . . . the pair are lost in an amazement of love and friendship and intimacy . . .

Love, friendship and intimacy occur within *both* romantic and platonic relationships. (Intimacy is just another word for vulnerability.) Romance features a fourth contributor: passion.

In a romantic relationship you typically expect and deserve passion, attraction and sex (unless you're an asexual honey), and sometimes monogamous commitment. Platonic love takes the physical and sexual out of the equation, yet it still promises closeness, acceptance, commitment and proactiveness.

Do not limit yourself by thinking love can only exist romantically. Love and connection with your platonic soulmate can inspire your mind, heart and soul and inspire you towards a version of yourself you're proud to be.

Humans gatekeep the word 'love' too much. We reserve it for a standard that may not necessarily exist. Personally, we say 'love you' every time we finish a phone call with each other.

Free yourself from the idea that you cannot dish out love like Oprah Winfrey dished out cars.

You get love.

You get *love*.

You. Get. Love.

One of our idols, Florence Given, whom we discussed in Chapter 1, coined the term 'living deliciously'. She prides herself on living joyfully and loving the little things in life. No overthinking, no questioning, just loving things she feels like loving. She loves matching her nails to her outfit, she loves looking at the colour in her day. She loves little and big.

Start loving your friendships, both little and big.

Movies, books, TV shows and other forms of pop culture unsurprisingly focus on romantic soulmates. We've seen a multitude of characters with their witty sidekick best friend who's there for comic relief to support the angsty main character and whoever they've got it bad for.

Until Meredith Grey and Cristina Yang from *Grey's Anatomy* entered the group chat.

'You're my person.'

The words are said in the dingy bar when Cristina, a very guarded, stubborn and independent person, tells Meredith she's put her down as her emergency contact for an emergency medical procedure she's scheduled.

Meredith simply responds 'I am?', knowing what this means. It's not about being her emergency contact. It's about being the person she turns to when she needs someone. It's about how Meredith understands Cristina for everything she is and will be, and still chooses to love her.

This theme never fades throughout their friendship. 'If I murdered someone, she's the person I'd call to help drag the corpse across the living room floor,' Cristina says.

Their connection is not woven by blood or by a ring on the fourth finger. Instead, we see two friends who without each other are a little less. But together? Everything and more.

We personally can't think of a better way to describe platonic soulmates than having 'your person'. Because your platonic soulmate is the first person you want to call when you get the promotion at work. They're also the first person you want to call crying when your boss was an absolute arsehole.

Your platonic soulmate is someone you want to invite into your life and share it with, because they make the wins taste even sweeter and the lows just a shitty thing that happened last week.

The ability to connect to our friends on a deep level is literally built into our brains. So why fight it? It has been scientifically proven that we're likely to have similar brain patterns to our close friends. In a study published in the journal *Nature Communications*, a group of brain researchers and social psychologists studied a group of 42 students. They monitored their reactions as they watched some clips and MRI scans showed that friends who watched the same clips reacted in extremely similar ways. Just by observing how the different areas of the brain lit up, the researchers could predict who were and weren't friends within the group. (We often feel like our brains have morphed into one, so this checks out.)

Maybe we relate to the idea that friends can be soulmates so deeply because we've always thought of ourselves as twin flames.

We share a lot of similarities that showcase our soulmate status. Yet on a deeper level, it's our complementary differences that truly connect us. We're like two sides of the same coin. Fire and ice. Pleasure and pain. You can't have one without the other. That's because your soulmate is someone who completes you. While your interests and personality traits may be aligned, your friend will often possess amazing qualities that inspire you to be a better person. And maybe their flaws balance out with some of *your* amazing qualities. Your soulmate isn't just a carbon copy of yourself.

For example, you might be the friend who books the girls' trip, plans the entire itinerary and presents it in a beautifully colour-coded spreadsheet. You have amazing initiative, you're reliable and thoughtful. However, maybe you're also a *little* bit neurotic and don't cope well when life gets unpredictable. Your soulmate may be a little bit more relaxed and happy to go with the flow. However, they're going to be the one to push you out of your comfort zone and convince you to have drinks at that amazing bar rec they picked up from a local. They'll help you let go of your inhibitions and loosen the reins just that little bit to help you have more fun in the moment.

Despite your differences, your soulmate doesn't judge your flaws. You both have your strengths and areas in which you may be lacking, but together you create an unbeatable force.

Once you've met your soulmate, you won't be able to imagine life without them. You'll be convinced that every interaction before led you to each other, like some cosmic social butterfly effect. Personally, we wouldn't be surprised if our friendship exists in other realms. If we live in other timelines or universes, we'd be best friends there, too. We're also convinced that we'll be hosting season 86 of *Two Broke Biddies* (rebrand!) from our conjoined rooms in the retirement village. Al will be shamelessly hitting on the young nurses and Sal will be playing eighties rock on vinyl and telling everyone about the 'good ol' days'.

You can also have more than one soulmate. We're taught that there is one person out there for everyone, but we feel a little shortchanged by that notion. As humans, we have so much love to give that it seems a shame to limit ourselves to sharing such a beautiful bond with only one other person, out of the more than 8 billion people on earth. This is why, when you look back on your life so far, you may be able to think of a handful of people that you feel could fit in this special category for you. It's also why it's possible to have a soulmate in your romantic partner as well as your best friend simultaneously.

The exciting thing about this is that it works in the reverse. Your soulmate (or soulmates) could still be out there waiting for you. Maybe you just haven't found them yet. This is another reason why we think that it's so important not to close yourself off to making new friends when you're in your twenties and beyond. Who knows, your soulmate could be the barista near your new apartment building or that one chick you always share a smile with in your gym class. But you'll never know if you think, 'Oh, I already have my friends. I don't need any more' and don't embrace the opportunity for new people in your life. The same goes if you're too scared to put yourself out there due to fear of rejection.

What if you're reading this and thinking, 'I don't have a best friend' or 'I have lots of friends and acquaintances, but I don't know if I'd consider any of them soulmates'?

If you don't have that friend in your life who you consider your platonic other half, that's okay. Maybe your soulmate *is* your romantic partner. It could even be someone in your family. Even if you don't feel like you have that celestial connection with one particular friend, that doesn't diminish the validity of the friendships in your life. You don't *have* to have a platonic soulmate, but you can take comfort knowing that this type of friendship is possible and may still be in your future.

Eleven signs your friend is your platonic soulmate

How do you actually *know* if you've found a platonic soulmate in your friend? There could be an 'aha!' moment where it all clicks, or maybe it's something that you realise over time. The signs will also vary between friendships, but there are definitely some common traits to look out for.

1. They feel like home

This feeling will sneak up on you. You can't really pinpoint when it happened or how. When you're around this person your chest feels a little lighter, you breathe a bit easier and any noise in your head is a bit quieter. You realise that this person is actually one of the best parts of your life. That you don't have to make any effort for it to just 'work'.

A note from Al

I remember the exact moment I realised Sal was my soulmate—truly, deeply and without a doubt.

We'd been friends for a few years and she was truly my best friend in the whole world. We'd been through my bad break-up, some horrible bosses and a mountain of other things we helped each other through.

It was a night we'd lived dozens of times. We'd gotten ready at my apartment in a pair of band tees, watching a YouTube show of our two favourite drag queens, Trixie and Katya—Sal in a green eyeshadow look that I'd done for her, me in pink.

There is a simple perfection about getting ready with your best friend. You've got your favourite music playlist crackling through a rough-as-hell speaker; some Woolworths $4 brie, Jatz crackers and two for $6 dips, which is all definitely not enough to line your stomach; and a range of pre-drinks. It's one of those universal experiences that really should've been in the *Barbie* movie, but Greta and Margot are my idols so I'll let it slide. Somehow, your room always ends up looking like a bomb went off in it and at least one person has a menty-b about what they're going to wear. There have been so many nights in which we never made it out to an actual bar—we were just having way too much fun at pre-drinks. Just look at social media. 'Get ready with me' has become one of the most popular video themes. It put Alix Earle on the map, growing a following from 100,000 to 6 million within a year.

On this particular evening, we went to Frankie's in Sydney and danced the night away to a steady rotation of Queen, AC/DC and Bon Jovi. I remember watching Sal dance like she was in a music video and I knew I loved this girl.

Some people might find that odd to read. It might make them uncomfortable to say they're 'in love' with their friend, because we're taught that outside of our family, love is saved for a person we have a romantic, sexual relationship with.

Yes, there have been times people have joked that Sal and I are secretly in a romantic relationship, but it's because they don't understand the nature of a platonic soulmate connection.

In that underground rock'n'roll bar, I knew I would be there if she said, 'Bring a shovel and don't tell anyone,' and she would do the same for me. I knew if I asked her, 'Would you still love me if I was a worm?' her answer would be, 'Of course, I'd feed you little pieces of lettuce.' I knew that whatever happened in 20, 40, 60 years' time, we'd still be together.

I felt like I'd found a small piece of myself that I didn't know had been missing.

Yes, it all sounds very dramatic, but we're talking about soulmates here, people!

I knew on that crusty, dirty, sticky carpet floor that this chick and I were an endgame kind of thing, and I've never doubted it since.

2. You can spend quality time in silence together

Friends who can sit in silence together are elite. These friendships take very little from your social battery. In the best way possible, they are just as comfortable as spending time alone. There's no need to fill silences because they feel comfortable rather than awkward.

Our favourite form of this is lying in bed together, reading separate books. When we interviewed our friend Jemma Sbeg (host of the amazing podcast *The Psychology of Your 20s*—check it out!) for the podcast, she explained that this is called 'parallel play'. Initially our juvenile minds went somewhere in the gutter, but apparently it's a common term to describe how children learn how to play and socialise with one another. It's a completely valid form of social interaction that involves playing adjacent to each other but not *with* each other.

Personally, we believe the ability to parallel play in silence is a sign that your friend could be a platonic soulmate. Just like when you're spending time alone, you don't feel like you have to perform or entertain one another. You can just exist in your mate's company and it still feels like quality time spent together, even if nothing is said.

3. You feel seen as your authentic self

Do you ever feel like you're donning different personas with different friends? It's not that you're being fake or inauthentic—certain parts of your personality might just come through more prominently when you're with specific people. You might have a friend who brings out a more serious side in you, while with others you feel like you need to 'turn it on' and be the class clown. But with your platonic soulmate, you can show all sides of your personality and truly feel like yourself. When they ask 'How are you?' you actually say how you feel (even when you feel like a shit sandwich). That's because these friends accept you for everything you are: flaws, bad days and all.

You can share your deepest fears and biggest dreams with this person without fear of judgement or question. You can talk about anything with this person, because you feel so comfortable around each other. As a duo, you've helped each other grow and learned more about your true selves in the process.

4. When you're apart for too long, you don't feel whole

If you're used to seeing or speaking to this friend regularly, it can feel like you're missing a limb if it's too long between catch-ups. You're used to sharing everything from the mundane of every day to the milestone moments with this person. So when you're apart from one another, it feels like you're missing a part of yourself.

A note from Sal

The first of the 2020 lockdowns was a brutal reminder to all of us of how painful it can feel to be apart from those we love.

At the time, Al and I were around three years into our friendship, and probably at the peak of our once arguably unhealthy dependence on one another. Maybe 'unhealthy' is a dramatic term, but the amount of time we were spending together probably wasn't super sustainable. We would spend all day at work together and then go to the gym together. Then, if we weren't having a midweek slumber party, we'd spend our whole evening texting, Snapchatting and DMing each other on Instagram. Then we'd spend our weekends going out together. You get the picture. We were basically glued at the hip.

A week or so before shit got real and lockdown rumours started whirling, Alex stayed at my place and we worked on a puzzle with my boyfriend Chris. We got around halfway through in her time with us. Alex requested that, even if we worked on it some more, we not finish the puzzle without her. Obviously we agreed. But then we went into lockdown.

As we live on opposite sides of Sydney, Al and I couldn't even catch up for the government-mandated picnics or walks. We went from spending almost every second together to being apart for months. Chris and I slowly continued working on the puzzle (as people did in lockdown) but, as promised, we never finished it. We left one piece aside for Alex to pop in when she came over next. Like the most heavy-handed metaphor ever, we left that unfinished puzzle sitting on our coffee table for two months ready for Al to complete. Eventually, we realised the lockdown wasn't going to finish any time soon, and with Al's permission, we packed the puzzle away.

While we didn't feel quite whole when forced to spend so much time apart, the lockdowns didn't do anything to weaken our bond. It just forced us into a different era of our friendship. We had to become more independent and navigate a new dynamic where we couldn't rely on one another being there physically 24/7. Being apart felt a little like being homesick when you're on a long trip away. But we learned to deal with it. I think it helped us appreciate what we have and achieve a healthier balance that made our friendship even stronger.

5. You have your own language

This doesn't mean that you and your friend have created your own dialect of Dothraki or something (although, mad respect if you have). By this we mean you and your platonic soulmate communicate with each other in your own special way that's unique to your friendship. You finish each other's sentences and can seemingly communicate telepathically. It's almost like you immediately know what the other is thinking, like your conversation is a backup version of your own internal dialogue. You also have a rolodex of inside jokes that no other sane person would find remotely funny.

In our case? We communicate largely via quotes from *The Grinch* and *Thank God You're Here*–style improvisation. When we worked together at our old job, people would often look at us with a mixture of awe and horror. One would make the other laugh and that would result in a five-minute-long comedic bit that sounded like the world's most obnoxious laugh, the sound of a Tasmanian devil and our very own form of gibberish were chucked in a blender. A lot of the time we'd receive eye-rolls but occasionally someone would be brave enough to jump in and play along with us, to our great delight.

6. You don't judge each other's pasts or mistakes

Your soulmate understands that you're human and will make mistakes. They don't constantly bring up your past not-so-great behaviour to embarrass you or make you feel ashamed. And if they do, it's because they're trying to show you how far you've come or help you stop history from repeating itself.

Your soulmate won't look the other way when you're being a little shit, though. If they see that you're self-sabotaging with shady behaviour, they'll pull you up on it. Not to berate or belittle you, but because they want you to be the best version of yourself. When you do fuck up (which, let's be real, we all do), they're ready to listen and give advice without judgement.

7. You've weathered storms together

Having a platonic soulmate doesn't mean that your relationship is perfect and nothing but personal jokes and happy memories. It also means that you've endured hardships together and come out the other side stronger. You might've supported one another through a particularly tough time, from break-ups and toxic workplaces to grief and mental health struggles. When things are rough for your friend, you feel their pain more deeply than you do with your other friends—almost as if it were your own.

Your friendship may have even experienced conflicts of its own, but you've both made the effort to resolve it together. There are obviously a lot of factors at play, but true soulmates will withstand the hard times in honour of the good.

8. You genuinely celebrate each other's wins

Just like you feel your soulmate's heartbreaks as if they're your own, you always celebrate their wins as if they were yours. You're their biggest cheerleader in all areas of life and vice versa. This is because it makes you genuinely happy to see them succeeding and living their best life. Unlike other more insecure friendships, you don't feel threatened or jealous when you see them thriving. In a similar way, this person is one of the first people you call when you get amazing news. You want to share the moment with them because you know they'll be sincerely over the moon for you, they'll support you and ask you questions because they actually want to know more. All without a hint of resentment.

9. Your favourite memories are shared with them

When you flick through the photo album of core memories in your mind, this friend is a recurring character. From wild birthday parties to adventures in overseas cities and days spent on the couch binge-watching your favourite reality TV show, you can always rely on them to be by your side and contribute to having a hell of a time. When you think ahead to the big events in your future, you imagine how they'll fit into the picture, too.

10. They appeared in your life when you needed them

How you met your platonic soulmate can sometimes feel like fate—as if the universe pushed you together in pursuit of a greater plan. Perhaps it was on the first day of high school, to give you a sidekick to prepare for the six years of adolescent hell ahead. Or it could've been during a time in your life when you were dating an absolute crumb of a human and your self-esteem was in the toilet. In this instance, the universe clearly knew that you needed someone to remind you of the absolute queen that you are and that it's time to dump their arse.

Because life isn't a rom-com, the first time you meet your person probably won't be a well-lit moment that stops time and is backed by some perfectly timed early 2000s slow jam. You'll probably click immediately but it might not hit you that you've met your platonic soulmate right away. But when you look back on the picture of your life, we bet you can pinpoint exactly why this person entered your life when they did.

11. You grow together

You wouldn't be the person you are today without this friend. Rather than agreeing on everything for the sake of it, you've challenged each other to consider different opinions. They encourage you to step out of your comfort zone and inspire you to do things a little differently.

You've also learned a lot from the stories they've shared and the unique way they see the world.

The friendship has also taught you both about loyalty, compassion and unconditional love. Your friend has shown you that there are people in the world you can trust wholeheartedly and who will love you even at your lowest moments. Which is probably a lot, considering some of the hangry, unhinged and hungover versions of yourself they've likely witnessed.

It's not that one person is forcing the other to grow up or change personalities to assimilate with theirs, either. It's a mutual exchange that benefits you both.

If a particular (or maybe more than one) person popped into your head as you read through this chapter, you should tell them. If flowery confessions of love of Shakespearean proportions aren't your thing, that's okay. You can tell them in your own way.

Even if you're the type of friends who usually communicate exclusively via sarcasm and digs at each other, an odd moment of sincerity never hurt anyone. In fact, even if they cringe at first, we bet deep down they'll really appreciate it.

You can reserve it for a special moment like inside their next birthday card or when you're thanking them after they've really gone out of their way to do something for you. Our personal favourite is when you're feeling extra lovey dovey after taking advantage of a good ol' happy hour down at the local. We know we said never to handle conflict with friends under the influence, but confessions of love are a different ball game, baby. Let the wholesome D&Ms flow, we say. However you decide to do it, it is important to show and tell the people in your life that you appreciate them.

Personally, we love blurting this out to one another in the moment and exactly as we're feeling it. In the history of our friendship, this conversation has happened in nail salon chairs, sweaty dive bar dance floors and across Slack IMs. Professional, we know! But whatever. We're each other's soulmates and we're not afraid to say it. In fact, it feels fuckin' good whenever we do.

So next time you start getting that warm and fuzzy feeling about that special friend in your life, turn to them and tell them you love 'em. You won't regret it.

OUR WISH FOR YOU, OUR NEW FRIEND

EPILOGUE

Our wish is that you find your people, and that when you do it feels like something has clicked into place—like you've known them all your life.

We hope you find people who make the hard things in life feel a little bit easier. People who heal things within you they didn't even break. People who bring you an almond croissant just because they know you like them. People who send you a link to an online sale because they know you need a new pair of jeans. People who grab you a chocolate at the checkout just 'cos. People who personify the Seven Friend Theory, or help you believe in soulmates.

We wish for you to find people who will hold your hand when you cry, hold your hair back after too many cocktails and hold your head up for you when you need a confidence boost.

We know you deserve people who will feed your cat and empty its litterbox full of shit when you go on holiday; who will help you prepare for an interview for your dream job; who will win when you win and lose when you lose.

We hope you find people with whom you develop your own kind of language, or can communicate with using a side-eye glance. They know when something is wrong but never push. They love all of you with all of their heart.

It's okay if you don't know these people yet. They won't all come at once.

They'll come when you're at a bar dancing to a niche song that only you like because of some silly backstory. They'll come when you make small talk at a random party and end up chatting into the early hours of the night. You'll find them in the cubicle next to you at work, or on a much-needed coffee run.

Every day people flow in and out of your life, but your people are the ones who stick. They may be with you for weeks, months or years. They may come in and out of your life. Or, if you're lucky, they may stick around forever.

Every day of the rest of your life is another day in which you could find your people. How fucking cool is that?

Lots of love,

Sal and Al

ACKNOWLEDGEMENTS

The following pages would not have been possible without the family and friendships that have inspired them. To our friends old and new, you know who you are and we couldn't have done this without the memories we've shared, your gems of wisdom and the many incredible lessons you have taught us.

We would also love to thank our partners Chris and Rob for their ongoing support and love during the many months of late nights, pep talks and countless iced lattes it took to write this book.

We're so grateful for Tessa Feggans and the team at Allen & Unwin for their constant guidance and unwavering belief in us and the vision we had for this book.

Last but not least, we need to thank *The Chicks*. Whether you've listened to the podcast, stumbled across us on social media or have been with us on this journey since the very beginning: Finding Your People is our gift to you. We owe every opportunity we've had to your support of *Two Broke Chicks* and many of the following chapters are shaped by the questions and life lessons you've so graciously shared with us. We hope this book can be a friend to lean on and ultimately helps you find your people.

CHAPTER SOURCES

Soooo, do you wanna be friends?

p. 4: Solan, M., 2017, 'The secret to happiness? Here's some advice from the longest-running study on happiness', *Harvard Health Blog*, <www.health.harvard.edu/blog/the-secret-to-happiness-heres-some-advice-from-the-longest-running-study-on-happiness-2017100512543>, accessed 9 January 2024

p. 4: Koudstaal, S., 2022, 'Social isolation and susceptibility for developing heart failure: are we exchanging a global pandemic for a new crisis in the making?', *European Heart Journal Open*, vol. 2, no. 1

Chapter 1: Be your own bestie

p. 21: Bloom, S., n.d., 'How we spend our time', <www.sahilbloom.com/newsletter/how-we-spend-our-time>, accessed 9 January 2024

p. 31: Shetty, J., 2021, 'Jay Shetty on 8 ways to deal with negativity', *Jay Shetty*, <www.jayshetty.me/blog/jay-shetty-on-8-ways-to-deal-with-negativity>, accessed 9 January 2024

Chapter 2: A reason, a season or a lifetime

p. 55: Netherlands Organization for Scientific Research, 2009, 'Half Of Your Friends Lost In Seven Years, Social Network Study Finds', *ScienceDaily*, <www.sciencedaily.com/releases/2009/05/090527111907.htm>, accessed 9 January 2024

p. 63: George, K. & Schneider, C.M., 2022, '4 tips to stay connected when your friends live far away', *wbur*, <www.wbur.org/npr/1086433752/stay-connected-long-distance-friends>, accessed 9 January 2024

p. 71: Pearson, C., 2022, 'How Many Friends Do You Really Need?', *The New York Times*, <www.nytimes.com/2022/05/07/well/live/adult-friendships-number.html>, accessed 9 January 2024

Chapter 3: Friendship love languages

p. 83: Chapman, G., 1992, *The Five Love Languages: How to express heartfelt commitment to your mate*, Northfield Publishing

Chapter 4: Making friends in adulthood

p. 110: Hronis, A., 2022, 'Why do we find making new friends so hard as adults?', <www.uts.edu.au/news/health-science/why-do-we-find-making-new-friends-so-hard-adults>, accessed 8 February 2024

p. 116: Dunbar, R.I.M., 1992, 'Neocortex size as a constraint on group size in primates', *Journal of Human Evolution*, vol. 22, no. 6, pp. 469–93

p. 116: Suzanne Degges-White, S. & Kepic, M., 2020, 'Friendships, Subjective Age, and Life Satisfaction of Women in Midlife', *Adultspan Journal*, vol. 19, no. 1, pp. 39–53

p. 117: Snapchat, 2019, 'Celebrating Friendship with the Friendship Report', <https://newsroom.snap.com/friendship-report-2019>, accessed 9 January 2024

p. 127: McCay, J., 2023, 'The Top Causes of Stress', Compare the Market, <www.comparethemarket.com.au/health-insurance/features/top-causes-of-stress>, accessed 9 January 2024

p. 129: Neeson, M., n.d., 'Up to 3.4 million Australian workers say they dislike their manager', ACAP, <www.acap.edu.au/news-and-opinion/up-to-3-4-million-australian-workers-say-they-dislike-their-manager>, accessed 9 January 2024

p. 141: Lusinski, N., 2023 'How your attachment style affects your friendships', The Zoe Report, <https://thezoereport/wellness/how_attachment_styles_affect_your_friendships> accessed 29 Februrary 2024

Chapter 5: It's not always daisies, sparkles and unicorn farts

p. 154: Gilchrist-Petty, E. & Bennett, L.K., 2019, 'Cross-Sex Best Friendships and the Experience and Expression of Jealousy within Romantic Relationships', *Journal of Relationships Research*, vol. 10, no. 18

p. 162: *The Everygirl*, 2020, 'The Do's and Don'ts of Handling Conflict With a Friend', <https://theeverygirl.com/how-to-handle-conflict-with-a-friend>, accessed 9 January 2024

p. 169: Lewicki, R.J., Polin, B. & Lount, R.B., 2016, 'An Exploration of the Structure of Effective Apologies', *Negotiation and Conflict Management Research*, vol. 9, no. 2, pp. 177–96

p. 170: Chapman, G. & Thomas, J. 2009, *Five Languages of Apology*, Jaico Publishing House

Chapter 6: Toxic friendships

p. 193: Robbins, M.L. & Karan, A., 2019, 'Who Gossips and How in Everyday Life?', *Social Psychological and Personality Science*, vol. 11, no. 2

p. 196: Carmichael, C.L., Reis, H.T. & Duberstein, P.R., 2015, 'In Your 20s it's Quantity, in Your 30s it's Quality: The Prognostic Value of Social Activity Across 30 Years of Adulthood', *Psychology and Aging*, vol. 30, no. 1, pp. 95–105

p. 201: Janis, I., 'Groupthink', *Psychology Today*, <https://www.psychologytoday.com/au/basics/groupthink>, accessed 8 February 2024

Chapter 7: Friendships versus romantic relationships

p. 215: Seidman, G., 2018, 'Is Social Media PDA a Sign of Happiness or Overcompensation?', *Psychology Today*, <www.psychologytoday.com/au/blog/close-encounters/201811/is-social-media-pda-sign-happiness-or-overcompensation>, accessed 9 January 2024

p. 217: Adamczyk, K. & Segrin, C., 2014, 'Perceived Social Support and Mental Health Among Young Single vs. Partnered Polish Young Adults', *Current Psychol*, vol. 34, pp. 82–96, <www.ncbi.nlm.nih.gov/pmc/articles/PMC4348549/#:~:text=Results%20indicated%20that%20single%20individuals,well%20in%20total%20well%2Dbeing>, accessed 8 February 2024

Chapter 8: Friendship dates

p. 247: Unknown, 2022, 'Can brisk walking reduce your biological age?', <www.bhf.org.uk/informationsupport/heart-matters-magazine/news/behind-the-headlines/can-brisk-walking-reduce-your-biological-age>, accessed 8 February 2024

p. 249: Wallace, J.P., Raglin, J.S. & Jastremski, C.A., 1995, 'Twelve month adherence of adults who joined a fitness program with a spouse vs without a spouse', *J Sports Med Phys Fitness*, vol. 35, no. 3, pp. 206–13.

p. 249: MacEwan University, 2016, 'Benefits of small group training', <https://sites-dev.macewan.ca/devsportsandwellness2/2016/02/02/benefits-of-small-group-training>, accessed 9 January 2024

Chapter 9: Life lessons from iconic besties

p. 262: Loudenback, T., 2021, 'A survey of 2,000 Americans found they're more likely to talk about politics and relationships with their friends than money', *Business Insider*, <www.businessinsider.com/data-americans-dont-talk-about-money-with-friends-2021-6>, accessed 9 January 2024

p. 263: Palmer, F., 2016, 'This is exactly how much money Joey owes Chandler in Friends', *Marie Claire*, <www.marieclaire.co.uk/entertainment/tv-and-film/friends-joey-owes-chandler-this-much-money-421531>, accessed 9 January 2024

Chapter 10: Finding your soulmate

p. 283: Hendley, S., 2021, 'What is a platonic soulmate? Here's how to know if you've found yours', *Body and Soul*, <www.bodyandsoul.com.au/sex-relationships/relationships/what-is-a-platonic-soulmate-heres-how-to-know-if-youve-found-yours/news-story/cbd14cae3a88acf30e137e9709ca4d16>, accessed 9 January 2024

p. 284: Plato, 381, *The Symposium*.

p. 287: Brueck, H., 2018, 'Scientists say they can predict who you're friends with based on brain patterns alone', *Business Insider*, <www.businessinsider.com/brains-friends-are-more-alike-scientists-say-2018-1>, accessed 9 January 2024